1 Crust, 100 Pizzas

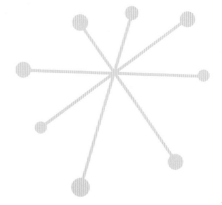

1 Crust, 100 Pizzas

Rachel Carter

First published in 2011
LOVE FOOD is an imprint of Parragon Books Ltd

Parragon
Queen Street House
4 Queen Street
Bath BA1 1HE, UK

ISBN: 978-1-4454-3320-2

Printed in China

Written by Rachel Carter
Photography by Mike Cooper
Home economy by Lincoln Jefferson

Notes for the Reader
This book uses imperial, metric, and US cup measurements.
Follow the same units of measurement throughout; do not mix
imperial and metric. All spoon measurements are level: teaspoons
are assumed to be 5 ml, and tablespoons are assumed to be 15 ml.
Unless otherwise stated, milk is assumed to be whole, eggs and
individual vegetables, such as potatoes, are medium, and pepper
is freshly ground black pepper.

The times given are an approximate guide only. Preparation times
differ according to the techniques used by different people and the
cooking times may also vary from those given as a result of the type
of oven used. Optional ingredients, variations, or serving suggestions
have not been included in the calculations.

Recipes using raw or very lightly cooked eggs should be avoided
by infants, the elderly, pregnant women, convalescents, and anyone
with a chronic condition. Pregnant and breast-feeding women are
advised to avoid eating peanuts and peanut products. People with
nut allergies should be aware that some of the prepared ingredients
used in the recipes in this book may contain nuts. Always check the
package before use.

Contents

6 Introduction

12 Vegetable Delights

54 Meat Lovers

96 Fish & Seafood

138 Nice & Spicy

180 Designer Pizzas

222 Index

Introduction

The origins of pizza are not clear cut; it seems that the idea was originally taken not from the Italians but the Greeks, who ate pieces of circular, flat bread flavored with oil, spices, and herbs. It wasn't until these breads found their way into the streets of Naples in the eighteenth century that they became known as pizzas. Their popularity rose when in the mid-1800s the Italian queen Margherita and her husband were traveling around Italy and fell in love with this popular street food. They were inspired to ask their chefs to work on different flavor combinations, using bread as the crust, and the ubiquitous margherita pizza was invented, using the colors of the Italian flag, with tomatoes, mozzarella, and fresh basil as the topping.

Of course, pizzas are now a world-wide phenomenon, and the choice of toppings is endless. This book features five chapters, starting with vegetable toppings, followed by meat-based pizzas, fish and seafood, spicy pizzas, and finally a designer pizzas chapter full of fun, unique ideas!

A basic recipe for the dough on page 10 forms the basis of all the recipes. Some of the dough will vary in size and shape and others will have additions of herbs or spices, but essentially it is the same recipe throughout. The basic dough recipe makes enough for two good-size thin crust pizzas, which will feed four, or will make one large, thicker crust version.

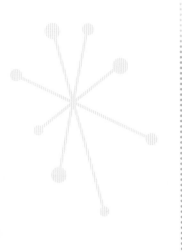

The Dough

When making pizza dough, the best and most authentic dough is a bread-based one, using yeast as the leavening agent. Instant yeast is sold in envelopes or jars and doesn't require dissolving in water. If you prefer to use fast active yeast or fresh yeast (the latter type is available to buy in good bakeries), you'll need to dissolve it with 1 teaspoon of sugar mixed with warm water and let it stand in a warm place for 20 minutes, until frothy. Once the yeast mixture is frothy, you can then follow the recipe in the normal way. Use the same amount of active dry yeast as a substitute for instant yeast, or one cake of fresh yeast for each envelope or 2¼ teaspoons of instant yeast.

The flour that you use is also key to a good dough. White bread flour is the best because it has a high gluten content, which produces a good rise during baking. You could also substitute white bread flour with whole wheat, whole-grain, spelt, or gluten-free versions.

The most common way of making pizza dough is to let it rise in a warm place for an hour or so to double in size. However, the yeast will still be effective if left in a cold place or refrigerator overnight. Any leftover dough can also be frozen and will still rise and cook normally when defrosted. Just wrap the dough tightly in plastic wrap and keep frozen for up to six months.

Kneading

Kneading the dough is the process that develops the gluten in the dough and encourages it to rise to produce a light textured bread. This vigorous method of stretching will typically take around 10 minutes if being kneaded by hand or about 3–5 minutes with an electric mixer and dough hook. You will know when the dough is ready because it will become smooth and very elastic.

A good way to test whether your dough is kneaded completely is to take a small piece of dough and do "the window test." Stretch the dough and if it is elastic and pulls apart without tearing, then it is ready. If it tears, continue kneading for a few more minutes.

Helpful Hints

If the dough becomes too wet during mixing, then just knead a little more flour into it. If it's very stretchy and difficult to roll out, then leave it for 10 minutes before trying again.

When rolling out the dough, use a rolling pin and keep turning it a quarter turn before rolling again until it reaches the required size. You'll find that you need far more pressure than when rolling pastry dough.

If you have a pizza stone, these are great for ensuring that the crust is completely cooked—just preheat it first. If you don't have one, use a preheated baking sheet. A pizza peel is a flat, wooden paddle used for getting pizzas on and off hot pizza stones. They can be useful but are by no means essential.

The basic dough recipe can also be used to make delicious garlic bread. Simply shape into a thick round after rising and drizzle with a little extra virgin olive oil and some sea salt and a little fresh chopped rosemary. Bake for 20–25 minutes and then brush with garlic butter.

If you want to get ahead, or when making pizzas in bulk, simply make the dough in advance, let it rise, then roll out, place on baking sheets, and cover with parchment paper until you are ready to use.

Pizza Sauce Recipe

The recipes in this book use prepared sauces as the base of the pizza. If you prefer to make your own, here is a quick recipe:-

1 tbsp olive oil

1 garlic clove, crushed

1 onion, finely chopped

14 oz/400 g canned chopped tomatoes

1 tbsp tomato paste

1 tsp dried oregano

salt and pepper

Heat the oil in a saucepan, add the garlic and onion, and sauté for 5–6 minutes, or until softened. Add the remaining ingredients and season to taste with salt and pepper. Simmer for abut 10 minutes, or until the mixture is reduced slightly, and suitable for spreading.

Homemade tomato pizza sauce can be stored in a screw-top jar in the refrigerator for up to a week.

You could also use strained pureed tomatoes, or even tomato paste, although this has a very intense flavor and is probably better diluted with a little water first. Peeled and finely diced fresh tomatoes may also be used, creating a different texture. Of course, not all pizzas include tomatoes or a tomato sauce. A great and tasty alternative is using pesto.

Basic Pizza Dough

**Makes two 10½-inch/26-cm round pizzas; or
four 7½-inch/19-cm round pizzas; or
one 15-inch x 10½-inch/38-cm x 26-cm rectangular pizza**

2¼ cups white bread flour, plus extra for dusting

1 tsp instant yeast

1½ tsp salt

¾ cup lukewarm water

1 tbsp olive oil, plus extra for kneading

1. Sift the flour into a mixing bowl and add the yeast and salt, making a small well in the top. Mix the water and oil together and pour into the bowl, using a round-blade knife to gradually combine all the flour to make a sticky dough.

2. Lightly flour the work surface and your hands and knead the dough for about 10 minutes, until it is smooth and elastic.

3. Cover the dough with some lightly oiled plastic or a damp dish towel and let rise for about an hour, or until it has doubled in size.

This is the basic recipe on which all 100 variations of pizzas in the book are based.

For each recipe, the basic mix is highlighted (*) for easy reference, so all you have to do is follow the easy steps each time and you'll never run out of ideas for tempting tasty pizzas!

Please note that the basic ingredients may vary from time to time, so please check these carefully.

Vegetable
Delights

Pizza Margherita

1. Make the pizza dough as described on page 10. Punch down the dough by gently kneading for about a minute, then divide into two balls. To roll out the dough, flatten each ball, then, using a rolling pin, roll out on a lightly floured work surface, giving a one-quarter turn between each roll.

2. Preheat the oven to 425°F/220°C. Place the pizza crusts on two baking sheets, using a rolling pin to transfer them from the work surface.

3. Divide the pizza sauce between the two pizza crusts, spreading almost to the edges. Scatter over the garlic and then top with the mozzarella cheese and Parmesan cheese. Season to taste with salt and pepper and drizzle over the olive oil.

4. Bake in the preheated oven for 10–12 minutes, or until the cheeses are melting and turning golden and the crusts are crisp underneath. Garnish with basil leaves and serve immediately.

Makes 2 pizzas

1 quantity Basic Pizza Dough

Topping
¾ cup prepared pizza sauce

2 garlic cloves, crushed

9 oz/250 g mozzarella cheese, drained and coarsely torn

1 oz/25 g Parmesan cheese, shaved

2 tbsp extra virgin olive oil

salt and pepper

fresh basil leaves, to garnish

Vegetable & Goat Cheese Pizza

1. Make the pizza dough as described on page 10. Punch down the dough by gently kneading for about a minute, then divide into two balls. To roll out the dough, flatten each ball, then, using a rolling pin, roll out on a lightly floured work surface, giving a one-quarter turn between each roll.

2. Preheat the oven to 425°F/220°C. Place the pizza crusts on two baking sheets, using a rolling pin to transfer them from the work surface.

3. Divide the pizza sauce between the two pizza crusts, spreading almost to the edges.

4. Heat half of the oil in a ridged grill pan over high heat until very hot. Add the garlic and zucchini and cook over medium heat for 4–5 minutes, turning regularly, until softened and charbroiled. Remove with a slotted spoon and drain on paper towels.

5. Add the remaining oil to the pan and repeat with the eggplant slices. Remove with a slotted spoon and drain on paper towels.

6. Scatter the zucchini and eggplant slices between the pizzas, top with the cheese, and season to taste with salt and pepper.

7. Bake in the preheated oven for 10–12 minutes, or until the cheese is melting and turning golden and the crusts are crisp underneath. Serve immediately.

Makes 2 pizzas

* 1 quantity Basic Pizza Dough

Topping
¾ cup prepared pizza sauce
2 tbsp olive oil
1 garlic clove, finely chopped
1 zucchini, thinly sliced lengthwise
1 small eggplant, thinly sliced lengthwise
7 oz/200 g soft goat cheese, thinly sliced
salt and pepper

Goat Cheese & Olive Pizza

1. Make the pizza dough as described on page 10. Punch down the dough by gently kneading for about a minute, then divide into two balls. To roll out the dough, flatten each ball, then, using a rolling pin, roll out on a lightly floured work surface, giving a quarter turn between each roll.

2. Preheat the oven to 425°F/220°C. Place the pizza crusts on two baking sheets, using a rolling pin to transfer them from the work surface.

3. Divide the pizza sauce between the two pizza crusts, spreading almost to the edges. Scatter over the tomatoes, olives, and cheese. Sprinkle over the herbs and season to taste with salt and pepper.

4. Bake in the preheated oven for 10–12 minutes, or until the cheese is melting and turning golden and the crusts are crisp underneath. Serve immediately.

Makes 2 pizzas

1 quantity Basic Pizza Dough

Topping
¾ cup prepared pizza sauce

8 cherry tomatoes, thinly sliced

⅓ cup thinly sliced, pitted black or green olives

7 oz/200 g soft goat cheese, thinly sliced

2 tsp herbes de provence

salt and pepper

Spinach, Egg & Olive Pizza

1. Make the pizza dough as described on page 10. Punch down the dough by gently kneading for about a minute, then divide into four balls. To roll out the dough, flatten each ball, then, using a rolling pin, roll out on a lightly floured work surface, giving a quarter turn between each roll.

2. Preheat the oven to 425°F/220°C. Place the pizza crusts on two baking sheets, using a rolling pin to transfer them from the work surface.

3. Put the spinach into a small saucepan, place over low heat, and cook for 1–2 minutes, or until it has wilted. Drain the spinach through a strainer and press down with the back of a spoon to remove any excess water.

4. Divide the pizza sauce among the four pizza crusts, spreading almost to the edges. Scatter over the garlic, top with the spinach and olives, and drizzle over the garlic oil.

5. Bake in the preheated oven for 8–10 minutes, then remove from the oven and make a small indentation in the center of each pizza. Pour an egg into each indentation, scatter over the cheese, and season to taste with salt and pepper. Return to the oven and bake for an additional 3–5 minutes, or until the eggs are just cooked and the crusts are crisp underneath. Serve immediately.

Makes 4 small pizzas

✳ 1 quantity Basic Pizza Dough

Topping
9 oz/250 g fresh spinach, washed and drained
¾ cup prepared pizza sauce
2 garlic cloves, finely chopped
¼ cup halved, pitted black olives
2 tbsp garlic olive oil
4 eggs
¾ cup finely grated Grana Padano cheese or Parmesan cheese
salt and pepper

Sicilian Pizza

1. Make the pizza dough as described on page 10. Punch down the dough by gently kneading for about a minute. Roll out the dough on a lightly floured work surface to a 15 x 10½-inch/ 38 x 26-cm rectangle.

2. Preheat the oven to 425°F/220°C. Place the pizza crust on a 15 x 10½-inch/38 x 26-cm baking sheet, using a rolling pin to transfer it from the work surface.

3. Spread the pizza sauce over the pizza crust, almost to the edges. Place the onion and red bell pepper pieces on one-quarter of the crust, the olives and capers on the next quarter, the mushrooms on the next, and the green bell pepper and artichoke pieces on the fourth quarter. Scatter over the cheese and season to taste with pepper.

4. Bake in the preheated oven for 15–20 minutes, or until the cheese is melting and turning golden and the crust is crisp underneath. Serve immediately

Makes 1 large pizza

* 1 quantity Basic Pizza Dough

Topping
¾ cup prepared pizza sauce

½ red onion, finely sliced

½ red bell pepper, seeded and finely sliced

¼ cup halved, pitted black olives

1 tbsp drained capers

1¼ cups sliced button mushrooms

½ green bell pepper, seeded and finely sliced

1¾ oz/50 g artichoke hearts in oil, drained and halved

9 oz/250 g mozzarella cheese, drained and coarsely torn

pepper

Artichoke & Brie Pizza

1. Make the pizza dough as described on page 10. Punch down the dough by gently kneading for about a minute, then divide into two balls. To roll out the dough, flatten each ball, then, using a rolling pin, roll out on a lightly floured work surface, giving a quarter turn between each roll.

2. Preheat the oven to 425°F/220°C. Place the pizza crusts on two baking sheets, using a rolling pin to transfer them from the work surface.

3. Divide the pizza sauce between the two pizza crusts, spreading almost to the edges. Scatter over the red onion and artichoke pieces, then top with the Brie. Scatter over the thyme, then drizzle with the reserved oil. Season to taste with salt and pepper.

4. Bake in the preheated oven for 10–12 minutes, or until the cheese is melting and turning golden and the crusts are crisp underneath. Serve immediately.

Makes 2 pizzas

* 1 quantity Basic Pizza Dough

Topping
¾ cup prepared pizza sauce
1 small red onion, finely sliced
7 oz/200 g artichoke hearts in oil, drained and cut into quarters, 1 tbsp oil reserved
9 oz/250 g Brie, thinly sliced
1½ tsp finely chopped fresh thyme leaves
salt and pepper

Garlic, Mushroom &
Gruyère Pizza

1. Make the pizza dough as described on page 10. Punch down the dough by gently kneading for about a minute, then divide into two balls. To roll out the dough, flatten each ball, then, using a rolling pin, roll out on a lightly floured work surface, giving a quarter turn between each roll.

2. Preheat the oven to 425°F/220°C. Place the pizza crusts on two baking sheets, using a rolling pin to transfer them from the work surface.

3. Divide the pizza sauce between the two pizza crusts, spreading almost to the edges.

4. Heat the oil in a skillet over medium heat, then add the garlic and mushrooms and sauté gently over medium heat for 4–5 minutes, until softened. Drain on paper towels and then scatter over the pizza crusts. Top with the cheese and season to taste with salt and pepper.

5. Bake in the preheated oven for 10–12 minutes, or until the cheese is melting and turning golden and the crusts are crisp underneath. Garnish with the chopped parsley and serve immediately.

Makes 2 pizzas

1 quantity Basic Pizza Dough

Topping
¾ cup prepared pizza sauce

1 tbsp olive oil

2 garlic cloves, crushed

6 oz/175 g large portobello mushrooms, wiped and thinly sliced

1⅔ cups grated Gruyère cheese

salt and pepper

chopped fresh flat-leaf parsley, to garnish

Four Cheese Pizza

1. Make the pizza dough as described on page 10. Punch down the dough by gently kneading for about a minute, then divide into two balls. To roll out the dough, flatten each ball, then, using a rolling pin, roll out on a lightly floured work surface, giving a quarter turn between each roll.

2. Preheat the oven to 425°F/220°C. Place the pizza crusts on two baking sheets, using a rolling pin to transfer them from the work surface.

3. Spread the pizza sauce over the pizza crust, spreading almost to the edges. Arrange the cheeses on the crust, with one type of cheese on each quarter.

4. Bake in the preheated oven for 10–12 minutes, or until the cheeses are melting and turning golden and the crusts are crisp underneath. Season to taste with pepper and serve immediately.

Makes 2 pizzas

* 1 quantity Basic Pizza Dough

Topping
¾ cup prepared pizza sauce

9 oz/250 g mozzarella cheese, drained and coarsely torn

¾ crumbled blue cheese

scant 1 cup grated cheddar cheese

3½ oz/100 g Brie, thinly sliced

pepper

Pine Nut & Raisin Pizza

1. Make the pizza dough as described on page 10. Punch down the dough by gently kneading for about a minute, then divide into two balls. To roll out the dough, flatten each ball, then, using a rolling pin, roll out on a lightly floured work surface, giving a quarter turn between each roll.

2. Preheat the oven to 425°F/220°C. Place the pizza crusts on two baking sheets, using a rolling pin to transfer them from the work surface.

3. Divide the pizza sauce between the two pizza crusts, spreading almost to the edges.

4. Place the raisins, onion, pine nuts, and capers in a small bowl with the oil and toss together well. Scatter evenly over the pizza crusts, then top with the cheese and season to taste with salt and pepper.

5. Bake in the preheated oven for 10–12 minutes, or until the cheese is melting and turning golden and the crusts are crisp underneath. Serve immediately.

Makes 2 pizzas

✳ 1 quantity Basic Pizza Dough

Topping
¾ cup prepared pizza sauce
⅓ cup raisins
1 small red onion, finely sliced
⅓ cup pine nuts
2 tbsp drained capers
1 tbsp extra virgin olive oil
9 oz/250 g mozzarella cheese, drained and roughly torn
salt and pepper

Sun-Dried Tomato & Ricotta Cheese Calzone

1. Make the pizza dough as described on page 10. Punch down the dough by gently kneading for about a minute, then divide into two balls. To roll out the dough, flatten each ball, then, using a rolling pin, roll out on a lightly floured work surface, giving a quarter turn between each roll.

2. Preheat the oven to 425°F/220°C. Place the pizza crusts on two baking sheets, using a rolling pin to transfer them from the work surface.

3. Divide the pizza sauce between the two pizza crusts, spreading almost to the edges. Scatter the tomatoes over one-half of each crust, then spoon the cheese evenly over the tomatoes. Sprinkle over the herbs and season to taste with salt and pepper.

4. Brush the edges of the crusts with a little water, then fold them over the filling to make two half-moon-shape calzones. Seal the edges all the way around by folding a little of the dough over and pinching the edges together. Make small holes in the top of each calzone with the tip of a sharp knife.

5. Bake in the preheated oven for 10–12 minutes, or until the tops are golden and the crusts are crisp underneath. Serve immediately.

Makes 2 calzones

* 1 quantity Basic Pizza Dough

Filling
¾ cup prepared pizza sauce
1⅓ cups drained and halved sun-dried tomatoes in oil
⅔ cup ricotta cheese
1 tsp dried mixed herbs
salt and pepper

Spicy Mozzarella Pizza

1. Make the pizza dough as described on page 10. Punch down the dough by gently kneading for about a minute, then divide into two balls. To roll out the dough, flatten each ball, then, using a rolling pin, roll out on a lightly floured work surface, giving a quarter turn between each roll.

2. Preheat the oven to 425°F/220°C. Place the pizza crusts on two baking sheets, using a rolling pin to transfer them from the work surface.

3. Divide the pizza sauce between the two pizza crusts, spreading almost to the edges. Scatter over the onion, olives, cheese, and chile flakes. Drizzle over the oil and season to taste with salt and pepper.

4. Bake in the preheated oven for 10–12 minutes, or until the cheese is melting and turning golden and the crusts are crisp underneath. Serve immediately.

Makes 2 pizzas

1 quantity Basic Pizza Dough

Topping
¾ cup prepared pizza sauce

1 small red onion, finely sliced

¼ cup halved, pitted mixed olives

9 oz/250 g buffalo mozzarella cheese, drained and coarsely torn

½ tsp dried chile flakes

2 tsp extra virgin olive oil

salt and pepper

Vegetable Lovers Pizza

1. Make the pizza dough as described on page 10. Punch down the dough by gently kneading for about a minute, then divide into two balls. To roll out the dough, flatten each ball, then, using a rolling pin, roll out on a lightly floured work surface, giving a quarter turn between each roll.

2. Preheat the oven to 425°F/220°C. Place the pizza crusts on two baking sheets, using a rolling pin to transfer them from the work surface.

3. Bring a small saucepan of lightly salted water to a boil. Add the asparagus spears and cook for 2–3 minutes. Drain and plunge into ice cold water for 1–2 minutes (to retain the bright green color). Drain well.

4. Divide the pizza sauce between the two pizza crusts, spreading almost to the edges. Place the cooked asparagus all around the pizza crusts with the cut ends at the outside edges and the tips in the center. Scatter over the remaining vegetables and olives and the top with the cheese. Season to taste with salt and pepper.

5. Bake in the preheated oven for 12–15 minutes, or until the cheese is melting and turning golden and the crusts are crisp underneath. Serve immediately.

Makes 2 pizzas

※ 1 quantity Basic Pizza Dough

Topping
5½ oz/150 g asparagus spears, trimmed

¾ cup prepared pizza sauce

6 oz/175 g artichoke hearts in oil, drained and quartered

scant 3 cups wiped and thinly sliced button mushrooms

8 cherry tomatoes, thinly sliced

½ cup halved, pitted mixed olives

9 oz/250 g mozzarella cheese, drained and roughly torn

salt and pepper

Caramelized Red Onion & Fennel Pizza

1. Make the pizza dough as described on page 10. Punch down the dough by gently kneading for about a minute, then divide into two balls. To roll out the dough, flatten each ball, then, using a rolling pin, roll out on a lightly floured work surface, giving a quarter turn between each roll.

2. Preheat the oven to 425°F/220°C. Place the pizza crusts on two baking sheets, using a rolling pin to transfer them from the work surface.

3. Heat half of the oil in a griddle pan over medium heat, add the fennel, and cook over medium–high heat for 4–5 minutes, turning regularly until turning golden and starting to char. Remove from the pan and drain on paper towels.

4. Add the remaining oil to the pan, then add the onion and cook for 3–4 minutes, until starting to caramelize. Remove from the pan and drain on paper towels.

5. Divide the pizza sauce between the two pizza crusts, spreading almost to the edges. Scatter the fennel and onion over the pizza crusts, top with the cheese, and season to taste with salt and pepper.

6. Bake in the preheated oven for 10–12 minutes, or until the cheese is melting and turning golden and the crusts are crisp underneath. Serve immediately.

Makes 2 pizzas

1 quantity Basic Pizza Dough

Topping

1½ tbsp olive oil

1 fennel bulb, trimmed and finely sliced

1 red onion, sliced into rings

¾ cup prepared pizza sauce

2½ cups grated cheddar cheese

salt and pepper

Roasted Red Pepper & Asparagus Pizza

1. Make the pizza dough as described on page 10. Punch down the dough by gently kneading for about a minute, then divide into two balls. To roll out the dough, flatten each ball, then, using a rolling pin, roll out on a lightly floured work surface, giving a quarter turn between each roll.

2. Preheat the oven to 425°F/220°C. Place the pizza crusts on two baking sheets, using a rolling pin to transfer them from the work surface.

3. Bring a small saucepan of lightly salted water to a boil. Add the asparagus spears and cook for 2–3 minutes. Drain and plunge into ice cold water for 1–2 minutes (to retain the bright green color). Drain well.

4. Divide the pizza sauce between the two pizza crusts, spreading almost to the edges. Scatter over the cooked asparagus, red bell pepper, and cheese. Season to taste with salt and pepper.

5. Bake in the preheated oven for 10–12 minutes, or until the cheese is melting and turning golden and the crusts are crisp underneath. Serve immediately.

Makes 2 pizzas

* 1 quantity Basic Pizza Dough

Topping
5½ oz/150 g asparagus spears, trimmed

¾ cup prepared pizza sauce

1 prepared roasted red bell pepper, drained and thinly sliced

9 oz/250 g mozzarella cheese, drained and coarsely torn

salt and pepper

Blue Cheese & Pear Pizza

1. Make the pizza dough as described on page 10. Punch down the dough by gently kneading for about a minute, then divide into two balls. To roll out the dough, flatten each ball, then, using a rolling pin, roll out on a lightly floured work surface, giving a quarter turn between each roll.

2. Preheat the oven to 425°F/220°C. Place the pizza crusts on two baking sheets, using a rolling pin to transfer them from the work surface.

3. Divide the pizza sauce between the two pizza crusts, spreading almost to the edges. Scatter over the pear slices, followed by the cheese. Season to taste with pepper.

4. Bake in the preheated oven for 10–12 minutes, or until the cheese is melting and turning golden and the crusts are crisp underneath. Garnish with the fresh watercress and serve immediately.

Makes 2 pizzas

1 quantity Basic Pizza Dough

Topping
¾ cup prepared pizza sauce

2 small ripe pears, cored and finely sliced

1½ cups crumbled Gorgonzola cheese or other blue cheese

pepper

fresh watercress, to garnish

Pizza Neapolitan

1. Make the pizza dough as described on page 10. Punch down the dough by gently kneading for about a minute, then divide into two balls. To roll out the dough, flatten each ball, then, using a rolling pin, roll out on a lightly floured work surface, giving a quarter turn between each roll.

2. Preheat the oven to 425°F/220°C. Place the pizza crusts on two baking sheets, using a rolling pin to transfer them from the work surface.

3. Divide the pizza sauce between the two pizza crusts, spreading almost to the edges. Scatter over the garlic, tomatoes, and the herb seasoning and drizzle over the oil. Season to taste with salt and pepper.

4. Bake in the preheated oven for 10–12 minutes, or until the crusts are crisp underneath. Garnish with the fresh basil and serve immediately.

Makes 2 pizzas

* 1 quantity Basic Pizza Dough

Topping
¾ cup prepared pizza sauce
2 garlic cloves, crushed
4 small tomatoes, thinly sliced
1 tsp dried Italian herb seasoning
1 tbsp extra virgin olive oil
salt and pepper
fresh basil leaves, coarsely torn, to garnish

17

Grilled Zucchini & Feta Pizza

1. Make the pizza dough as described on page 10. Punch down the dough by gently kneading for about a minute, then divide into two balls. To roll out the dough, flatten each ball, then, using a rolling pin, roll out on a lightly floured work surface, giving a quarter turn between each roll.

2. Preheat the oven to 425°F/220°C. Place the pizza crusts on two baking sheets, using a rolling pin to transfer them from the work surface.

3. Heat the oil in a ridged grill pan over medium heat. Add the garlic and zucchini and cook over medium heat for 4–5 minutes, turning regularly, until softened and charbroiled. Remove with a slotted spoon and drain on paper towels.

4. Divide the pizza sauce between the two pizza crusts, spreading almost to the edges. Place the zucchini slices on the pizza crusts, scatter with the cheese, and season to taste with salt and pepper.

5. Bake in the preheated oven for 10–12 minutes, or until the cheese is turning golden and the crusts are crisp underneath. Garnish with the fresh mint and serve immediately.

Makes 2 pizzas

1 quantity Basic Pizza Dough

Topping
1 tbsp olive oil

1 clove garlic, crushed

1 large zucchini, sliced lengthwise

¾ cup prepared pizza sauce

1⅔ cups drained and crumbled feta cheese

salt and pepper

fresh mint leaves, coarsely torn, to garnish

Pesto & Ricotta Cheese Pizza

1. Make the pizza dough as described on page 10, but add the oregano with the flour. Punch down the dough by gently kneading for about a minute, then divide into four small balls. To roll out the dough, flatten each ball, then, using a rolling pin, roll out on a lightly floured work surface, giving a quarter turn between each roll, until the rounds are 7½ inches/19 cm in diameter.

2. Preheat the oven to 425°F/220°C. Place the pizza crusts on two baking sheets, using a rolling pin to transfer them from the work surface.

3. Divide the pesto among the four pizza crusts, spreading almost to the edges. Add the ricotta cheese, then scatter with the tomatoes. Finish with the Parmesan cheese and season to taste with salt and pepper.

4. Bake in the preheated oven for 10–12 minutes, or until the cheese is melting and turning golden and the crusts are crisp underneath. Garnish with the fresh basil and serve immediately.

Makes 4 small pizzas

1 quantity Basic Pizza Dough
1 tsp dried oregano

Topping
½ cup prepared pesto
heaping ¾ cup ricotta cheese
6 small tomatoes, thinly sliced
⅔ cup grated Parmesan cheese
salt and pepper
fresh basil leaves, to garnish

Mozzarella & Basil Pizza

1. Make the pizza dough as described on page 10. Punch down the dough by gently kneading for about a minute, then divide into two balls. To roll out the dough, flatten each ball, then, using a rolling pin, roll out on a lightly floured work surface, giving a quarter turn between each roll.

2. Preheat the oven to 425°F/220°C. Place the pizza crusts on two baking sheets, using a rolling pin to transfer them from the work surface.

3. Divide the pizza sauce between the two pizza crusts, spreading almost to the edges. Scatter over the cheese and tomatoes. Drizzle with oil and season to taste with salt and pepper.

4. Bake in the preheated oven for 10–12 minutes, or until the cheese is melting and turning golden and the crusts are crisp underneath. Garnish with the fresh basil and serve immediately.

Makes 2 pizzas

✳ 1 quantity Basic Pizza Dough

Topping
¾ cup prepared pizza sauce

9 oz/250 g light mozzarella cheese, drained and coarsely torn

6 tomatoes, finely sliced

1 tbsp extra virgin olive oil

salt and pepper

fresh basil leaves, to garnish

20

Potato & Rosemary Pizza

1. Make the pizza dough as described on page 10. Punch down the dough by gently kneading for about a minute, then divide into two balls. To roll out the dough, flatten each ball, then, using a rolling pin, roll out on a lightly floured work surface, giving a quarter turn between each roll.

2. Preheat the oven to 425°F/220°C. Place the pizza crusts on two baking sheets, using a rolling pin to transfer them from the work surface.

3. Place the potato slices in a saucepan of cold water. Bring to a boil and cook for 2–3 minutes. Drain and refresh in a saucepan of cold water for a few minutes, then drain well on paper towels. Add the garlic, oil, and rosemary, season to taste with salt and pepper, and toss well. Cover and set aside.

4. Divide the pizza sauce between the two pizza crusts, spreading almost to the edges. Scatter over the potato slices and onion slices and top with the cheese.

5. Bake in the preheated oven for 10–12 minutes, or until the cheese is melting and turning golden and the crusts are crisp underneath. Serve immediately.

Makes 2 pizzas

1 quantity Basic Pizza Dough

Topping
2 potatoes, peeled and very finely sliced

2 garlic cloves, crushed

1 tbsp extra virgin olive oil

1 tsp dried rosemary

¾ cup prepared pizza sauce

½ red onion, finely sliced

7 oz/200 g soft goat cheese, thinly sliced

salt and pepper

Meat Lovers

21

Meat Feast Pizza

1. Make the pizza dough as described on page 10. Punch down the dough by gently kneading for about a minute, then divide into two balls. To roll out the dough, flatten each ball, then, using a rolling pin, roll out on a lightly floured work surface, giving a quarter turn between each roll.

2. Preheat the oven to 425°F/220°C. Place the pizza crusts on two baking sheets, using a rolling pin to transfer them from the work surface.

3. Divide the pizza sauce between the two pizza crusts, spreading almost to the edges. Scatter over the pastrami, ham, and pepperoni, top with the mushrooms and red bell pepper, and finish with the cheese and herbs.

4. Bake in the preheated oven for 10–15 minutes, or until the cheese is melting and turning golden and the crusts are crisp underneath. Serve immediately.

Makes 2 pizzas

1 quantity Basic Pizza Dough

Topping
¾ cup prepared pizza sauce

3¼ oz/90 g pastrami, coarsely chopped

3½ oz/100 g cooked, sliced ham, coarsely chopped

3½ oz/100 g pepperoni, thinly sliced

1½ cups thinly sliced mushrooms

½ red bell pepper, seeded and thinly sliced

1¾ cups grated cheddar cheese

¼ tsp dried herbes de Provence

22

Hawaiian Pizza

1. Make the pizza dough as described on page 10. Punch down the dough by gently kneading for about a minute, then divide into two balls. To roll out the dough, flatten each ball, then, using a rolling pin, roll out on a lightly floured work surface, giving a quarter turn between each roll.

2. Preheat the oven to 425°F/220°C. Place the pizza crusts on two baking sheets, using a rolling pin to transfer them from the work surface.

3. Divide the pizza sauce between the two pizza crusts, spreading almost to the edges. Scatter over the ham and pineapple and top with the mozzarella cheese and cheddar cheese.

4. Bake in the preheated oven for 10–12 minutes, or until the cheeses are melting and turning golden and the crusts are crisp underneath. Serve immediately.

Makes 2 pizzas

* 1 quantity Basic Pizza Dough

Topping
¾ cup prepared pizza sauce

7 oz/200 g cooked, sliced ham, coarsely chopped

⅔ cup small fresh pineapple chunks

4½ oz/125 g mozzarella cheese, drained and coarsely torn

scant 1 cup grated cheddar cheese

Piccante Pizza

1. Make the pizza dough as described on page 10. Punch down the dough by gently kneading for about a minute. Using a rolling pin, roll out the dough on a lightly floured work surface to a 15 inch x 10½-inch/38 x 26-cm rectangle.

2. Heat the oil in a medium saucepan over medium heat, then add the onion and garlic and gently sauté for 4–5 minutes, until starting to soften. Add the chiles and red bell pepper and cook for an additional 1–2 minutes, then add the beef and continue to sauté over medium–high heat for 4–5 minutes, until lightly browned all over.

3. Add the tomato paste and cook for 1 minute, stirring all the time. Stir in the water and season to taste with salt and pepper, then cover and simmer for 10–15 minutes, stirring occasionally until the meat is thoroughly cooked. Remove from the heat and let cool.

4. Preheat the oven to 450°F/230°C. Place the pizza crust on a 15 inch x 10½-inch/38 x 26-cm rectangular baking sheet, using a rolling pin to transfer it from the work surface. Spread the pizza sauce over the pizza crust, then top with the beef mixture and scatter over the cheeses.

5. Bake in the preheated oven for 15–20 minutes, or until the cheeses are melting and turning golden and the crust is crisp underneath. Serve immediately.

Makes 1 large pizza

1 quantity Basic Pizza Dough

Topping
1 tbsp vegetable oil
1 onion, finely chopped
2 garlic cloves, crushed
2 red chiles, seeded and finely chopped
1 red bell pepper, seeded and chopped
1lb 2 oz/500 g lean ground beef
2 tbsp tomato paste
scant 1 cup cold water
salt and pepper
¾ cup prepared pizza sauce
scant 1 cup grated cheddar cheese
4½ oz/125 g mozzarella cheese, drained and coarsely torn

Canadian Bacon, Baked Egg and Mozzarella Pizza

1. Make the pizza dough as described on page 10. Punch down the dough by gently kneading for about a minute, then divide into two balls. To roll out the dough, flatten each ball, then, using a rolling pin, roll out on a lightly floured work surface, giving a quarter turn between each roll.

2. Preheat the oven to 425°F/220°C. Place the pizza crusts on two baking sheets, using a rolling pin to transfer them from the work surface.

3. Divide the pizza sauce between the two pizza crusts, spreading almost to the edges. Scatter over the bacon, thyme, and half of the cheese.

4. Bake in the preheated oven for 8–10 minutes. Remove the pizzas from the oven and make a small indentation in the center of each one. Pour an egg into each indentation, top with the remaining cheese, and bake in the oven for an additional 3–5 minutes, or until the cheese is melting and turning golden and the crusts are crisp underneath. Serve immediately.

Makes 2 pizzas

1 quantity Basic Pizza Dough

Topping

¾ cup prepared pizza sauce

4½ oz/125 g Canadian bacon cubes or smoked bacon, finely chopped

¼ tsp dried thyme

9 oz/250 g mozzarella cheese, drained and coarsely torn

2 eggs

25

Prosciutto & Arugula Pizza

1. Make the pizza dough as described on page 10. Punch down the dough by gently kneading for about a minute, then divide into two balls. To roll out the dough, flatten each ball, then, using a rolling pin, roll out on a lightly floured work surface, giving a quarter turn between each roll.

2. Preheat the oven to 425°F/220°C. Place the pizza crusts on two baking sheets, using a rolling pin to transfer them from the work surface.

3. Divide the pizza sauce between the two pizza crusts, spreading almost to the edges. Scatter over the prosciutto and olives and top with the mozzarella cheese.

4. Bake in the preheated oven for 10–15 minutes, or until the cheese is melting and turning golden and the crusts are crisp underneath.

5. Remove from the oven, drizzle over the oil, season to taste with salt and pepper, and garnish with the arugula. Serve immediately.

Makes 2 pizzas

1 quantity Basic Pizza Dough

Topping

¾ cup prepared pizza sauce

7 oz/200 g thinly sliced prosciutto, torn into large pieces

½ cup halved, pitted mixed olives

9 oz/250 g buffalo mozzarella cheese, drained and coarsely torn

1 tbsp extra virgin olive oil

salt and pepper

fresh arugula leaves, to garnish

Barbecued Chicken Pizza

1. Make the pizza dough as described on page 10. Punch down the dough by gently kneading for about a minute, then divide into two balls. To roll out the dough, flatten each ball, then, using a rolling pin, roll out on a lightly floured work surface, giving a quarter turn between each roll.

2. Preheat the oven to 425°F/220°C. Place the pizza crusts on two baking sheets, using a rolling pin to transfer them from the work surface.

3. Divide the barbecue sauce between the two pizza crusts, spreading almost to the edges. Scatter over the chicken, green bell pepper, and scallions. Top with the cheddar cheese and mozzarella cheese and season to taste with salt and pepper.

4. Bake in the preheated oven for 10–12 minutes, or until the cheeses are melting and turning golden and the crusts are crisp underneath. Serve immediately.

Makes 2 Pizzas

✳ 1 quantity Basic Pizza Dough

Topping
¾ cup prepared smoky barbecue sauce

heaping 1 cup coarsely chopped cooked chicken

1 green bell pepper, seeded and finely sliced

6 scallions, trimmed and finely chopped

scant 1 cup grated cheddar cheese

3½ oz/100 g mozzarella cheese, drained and coarsely torn

salt and pepper

Melted Brie & Bacon Pizza

1. Make the pizza dough as described on page 10. Punch down the dough by gently kneading for about a minute, then divide into two balls. To roll out the dough, flatten each ball, then, using a rolling pin, roll out on a lightly floured work surface, giving a quarter turn between each roll.

2. Preheat the oven to 475°F/240°C. Place the pizza crusts on two baking sheets, using a rolling pin to transfer them from the work surface.

3. Divide the pizza sauce between the two pizza crusts, spreading almost to the edges. Scatter the bacon over the crusts and bake in the preheated oven for 6–8 minutes.

4. Remove the pizzas from the oven and lay the cheese over the top. Return to the oven for an additional 6–8 minutes, or until the cheese is melting and turning golden and the crusts are crisp underneath.

5. Season to taste with salt and pepper, garnish with the arugula leaves, and serve immediately.

Makes 2 pizzas

1 quantity Basic Pizza Dough

Topping
¾ cup prepared pizza sauce
7 oz/200 g Canadian bacon, finely chopped
9 oz/250 g Brie, thinly sliced
salt and pepper
fresh arugula leaves, to garnish

Italian Meat Special Pizza

1. Make the pizza dough as described on page 10. Punch down the dough by gently kneading for about a minute, then divide into two balls. To roll out the dough, flatten each ball, then, using a rolling pin, roll out on a lightly floured work surface, giving a quarter turn between each roll.

2. Preheat the oven to 425°F/220°C. Place the pizza crusts on two baking sheets, using a rolling pin to transfer them from the work surface.

3. Divide the pizza sauce between the two pizza crusts, spreading almost to the edges. Scatter over the salami, prosciutto, olives, and oregano, top with the cheese, and season to taste with pepper.

4. Bake in the preheated oven for 10–12 minutes, or until the cheese is melting and turning golden and the crusts are crisp underneath. Serve immediately.

Makes 2 pizzas

✳ 1 quantity Basic Pizza Dough

Topping
¾ cup prepared pizza sauce

4½ oz/125 g Italian salami, thinly sliced

4½ oz/125 g prosciutto, coarsely torn

½ cup halved, pitted mixed olives

½ tsp dried oregano

9 oz/250 g mozzarella cheese, drained and coarsely torn

pepper

Chorizo & Manchego Pizza

1. Make the pizza dough as described on page 10. Punch down the dough by gently kneading for about a minute, then divide into two balls. To roll out the dough, flatten each ball, then, using a rolling pin, roll out on a lightly floured work surface, giving a quarter turn between each roll.

2. Preheat the oven to 425°F/220°C. Place the pizza crusts on two baking sheets, using a rolling pin to transfer them from the work surface.

3. Divide the pizza sauce between the two pizza crusts, spreading almost to the edges. Scatter over the chorizo, red bell pepper, and olives and top with the cheese. Season to taste with pepper.

4. Bake in the preheated oven for 10–12 minutes, or until the cheese is melting and turning golden and the crusts are crisp underneath. Cover with foil for the last few minutes of cooking if the chorizo starts to brown too quickly. Serve immediately.

Makes 2 pizzas

* 1 quantity Basic Pizza Dough

Topping

¾ cup prepared pizza sauce

6 oz/175 g chorizo sausage, thinly sliced

1 large prepared roasted red bell pepper, drained and thinly sliced

½ cup drained and halved, pitted Spanish olives in garlic oil

scant 1 cup grated Manchego cheese

pepper

Pepperoni & Jalapeño Pizza

1. Make the pizza dough as described on page 10. Punch down the dough by gently kneading for about a minute, then divide into two balls. To roll out the dough, flatten each ball, then, using a rolling pin, roll out on a lightly floured work surface, giving a quarter turn between each roll.

2. Preheat the oven to 425°F/220°C. Place the pizza crusts on two baking sheets, using a rolling pin to transfer them from the work surface.

3. Divide the pizza sauce between the two pizza crusts, spreading almost to the edges. Scatter over the onion, pepperoni, jalapeño peppers, and yellow bell pepper. Top with the cheese and season to taste with pepper.

4. Bake in the preheated oven for 10–12 minutes, or until the cheese is melting and turning golden and the crusts are crisp underneath. Serve immediately.

Makes 2 pizzas

1 quantity Basic Pizza Dough

Topping
¾ cup prepared pizza sauce

1 small red onion, finely sliced

9 oz/250 g hot pepperoni sausage, thinly sliced

⅓ cup drained, sliced hot red jalapeño peppers in oil

1 yellow bell pepper, seeded and finely sliced

1⅓ cup grated cheddar cheese

pepper

31

Salami & Artichoke Pizza

1. Make the pizza dough as described on page 10. Punch down the dough by gently kneading for about a minute, then divide into two balls. To roll out the dough, flatten each ball, then, using a rolling pin, roll out on a lightly floured work surface, giving a quarter turn between each roll.

2. Preheat the oven to 425°F/220°C. Place the pizza crusts on two baking sheets, using a rolling pin to transfer them from the work surface.

3. Divide the pizza sauce between the two pizza crusts, spreading almost to the edges. Scatter over the salami, orange bell pepper, artichoke hearts, and oregano, then top with the cheese. Season to taste with salt and pepper.

4. Bake in the preheated oven for 10–12 minutes, or until the cheese is melting and turning golden and the crusts are crisp underneath. Serve immediately.

Makes 2 pizzas

* 1 quantity Basic Pizza Dough

Topping
¾ cup prepared pizza sauce

9 oz/250 g Italian salami, thinly sliced

1 orange bell pepper, seeded and finely sliced

5½ oz/150 g artichoke hearts in vegetable oil, drained and cut into quarters

½ tsp dried oregano

6 oz/175 g soft goat cheese, thinly sliced

salt and pepper

Chipotle Chicken Pizza

1. Make the pizza dough as described on page 10. Punch down the dough by gently kneading for about a minute, then divide into two balls. To roll out the dough, flatten each ball, then, using a rolling pin, roll out on a lightly floured work surface, giving a quarter turn between each roll.

2. Preheat the oven to 425°F/220°C. Place the pizza crusts on two baking sheets, using a rolling pin to transfer them from the work surface.

3. Divide the salsa between the two pizza crusts, spreading almost to the edges. Scatter over the chicken, green bell pepper, and jalapeño peppers, then drizzle over the chipotle paste. Top with the cheese and season to taste with salt and pepper.

4. Bake in the preheated oven for 10–12 minutes, or until the cheese is melting and turning golden and the crusts are crisp underneath. Serve immediately.

Makes 2 pizzas

✳ 1 quantity Basic Pizza Dough

Topping

⅔ cup prepared spicy tomato salsa

1¼ cups cooked chicken torn into strips

1 green bell pepper, seeded and finely sliced

⅓ cup drained, sliced hot red jalapeño peppers in oil

2 tsp chipotle paste

9 oz/250 g mozzarella cheese, drained and coarsely torn

salt and pepper

Ham, Mushroom & Olive Pizza

1. Make the pizza dough as described on page 10. Punch down the dough by gently kneading for about a minute, then divide into two balls. To roll out the dough, flatten each ball, then, using a rolling pin, roll out on a lightly floured work surface, giving a quarter turn between each roll.

2. Preheat the oven to 425°F/220°C. Place the pizza crusts on two baking sheets, using a rolling pin to transfer them from the work surface.

3. Divide the pizza sauce between the two pizza crusts, spreading almost to the edges. Scatter over the ham, olives, and mushrooms and top with the cheese. Season to taste with salt and pepper.

4. Bake in the preheated oven for 10–12 minutes, or until the cheese is melting and turning golden and the crusts are crisp underneath. Serve immediately.

Makes 2 pizzas

* 1 quantity Basic Pizza Dough

Topping
¾ cup prepared pizza sauce

6 oz/175 g sliced, cooked ham, torn into strips

½ cup halved, pitted mixed olives

1½ cups thinly sliced button mushrooms

150 g/5½ oz mozzarella cheese, drained and coarsely torn

salt and pepper

34

Pesto Chicken Pizza

1. Make the pizza dough as described on page 10. Punch down the dough by gently kneading for about a minute, then divide into two balls. To roll out the dough, flatten each ball, then, using a rolling pin, roll out on a lightly floured work surface, giving a quarter turn between each roll.

2. Preheat the oven to 425°F/220°C. Place the pizza crusts on two baking sheets, using a rolling pin to transfer them from the work surface.

3. Divide the pesto between the two pizza crusts, spreading almost to the edges. Scatter over the chicken, corn kernels, and tomatoes. Top with the cheese and season to taste with salt and pepper.

4. Bake in the preheated oven for 10–12 minutes, or until the cheese is melting and turning golden and the crusts are crisp underneath. Serve immediately.

Makes 2 pizzas

* 1 quantity Basic Pizza Dough

Topping
½ cup prepared pesto
1¼ cup cooked chicken torn into strips
scant ½ cup drained canned corn kernels
6 cherry tomatoes, thinly sliced
9 oz/250 g mozzarella cheese, drained and coarsely torn
salt and pepper

Duck & Plum Sauce Pizza

1. Make the pizza dough as described on page 10. Punch down the dough by gently kneading for about a minute, then divide into two balls. To roll out the dough, flatten each ball, then, using a rolling pin, roll out on a lightly floured work surface, giving a quarter turn between each roll.

2. Preheat the oven to 425°F/220°C. Place the pizza crusts on two baking sheets, using a rolling pin to transfer them from the work surface.

3. Place the duck breasts on a baking sheet. Score through the skin several times with a sharp knife and season to taste with half of the five-spice powder and with salt and pepper. Bake in the preheated oven for 15–20 minutes, or until the skin is crisp and the duck is cooked to your liking.

4. Remove the duck from the oven and let cool for 5 minutes, then slice into thin strips. Pour over 3 tablespoons of the plum sauce and toss well.

5. Divide the remaining plum sauce between the two pizza crusts, spreading almost to the edges. Scatter over the cooked duck, half of the scallions, and the remaining five-spice powder.

6. Bake in the preheated oven for 10–12 minutes, until the crusts are crisp underneath. Garnish with the cucumber and the remaining scallions and serve immediately.

Makes 2 pizzas

1 quantity Basic Pizza Dough

Topping
10 oz/280 g duck breasts
1 tsp five-spice powder
generous ¾ cup prepared plum sauce
1 tsp Chinese five-spice (available in speciality food stores)
salt and pepper
½ cucumber, finely sliced, to garnish

Grilled Sirloin
& Blue Cheese Pizza

1. Make the pizza dough as described on page 10. Punch down the dough by gently kneading for about a minute, then divide into two balls. To roll out the dough, flatten each ball, then, using a rolling pin, roll out on a lightly floured work surface, giving a quarter turn between each roll.

2. Preheat the oven to 425°F/220°C. Place the pizza crusts on two baking sheets, using a rolling pin to transfer them from the work surface.

3. Preheat the broiler to high, place the steak on a broiler rack, and broil for 9–10 minutes, turning once, or until cooked to your liking. Remove from the broiler, let rest for 5 minutes, then slice thinly.

4. Divide the salsa between the two pizza crusts, spreading almost to the edges. Top with the meat and cheese and season to taste with pepper.

5. Bake in the preheated oven for 10–12 minutes, or until the crusts are crisp underneath. Garnish with the fresh arugula and serve immediately.

Makes 2 pizzas

※ 1 quantity Basic Pizza Dough

Topping
9 oz/250 g sirloin or top round steak, trimmed of all visible fat

¾ cup prepared tomato salsa

1½ cups crumbled blue cheese, such as gorgonzola

pepper

fresh arugula leaves, to garnish

Artichoke Pizza

1. Make the pizza dough as described on page 10. Punch down the dough by gently kneading for about a minute. Using a rolling pin, roll out the dough to a 15 x 10½-inch/ 38 x 26-cm rectangle on a lightly floured work surface.

2. Preheat the oven to 450°F/230°C. Place the pizza crust on a 15 x 10½-inch/38 x 26-cm rectangular baking sheet, using a rolling pin to transfer it from the work surface.

3. Spread the pizza sauce on the pizza crust, spreading almost to the edges. Scatter over the garlic, ham, olives, artichoke hearts, and tomatoes. Drizzle over the reserved oil and top with the mozzarella cheese and Parmesan cheese. Season to taste with pepper.

4. Bake in the preheated oven for 10–12 minutes, or until the cheeses are melting and turning golden and the crust is crisp underneath. Serve immediately.

Makes 1 large pizza

* 1 quantity Basic Pizza Dough

Topping
¾ cup prepared pizza sauce

1 garlic clove, finely chopped

6 oz/175 g cooked ham, torn into strips

½ cup halved, pitted mixed olives

7 oz/200 g artichoke hearts in oil, drained and cut into quarters

1⅓ cups drained and halved sun-dried tomatoes in oil, reserving 1 tbsp oil

5½ oz/150 g mozzarella cheese, drained and coarsely torn

3½ oz/100 g Parmesan cheese, shaved

pepper

The Greek Pizza

1. Make the pizza dough as described on page 10. Punch down the dough by gently kneading for about a minute. Using a rolling pin, roll out the dough to a 15 x 10½-inch/ 38 x 26-cm rectangle on a lightly floured work surface.

2. Heat the oil in a saucepan over medium heat, then add the onion and garlic and gently sauté for 4–5 minutes, or until starting to soften. Add the ground lamb and continue to sauté over medium–high heat for 4–5 minutes, until lightly browned all over.

3. Add the tomato paste and cook for 1 minute, stirring continuously. Add the eggplant, oregano, half of the pine nuts, and the water and season to taste with salt and pepper. Cover and simmer for 10–15 minutes, stirring occasionally, until the meat is thoroughly cooked. Remove from the heat and let cool.

4. Preheat the oven to 450°F/230°C. Place the pizza crust on a 15 x 10½-inch/38 x 26-cm rectangular baking sheet, using a rolling pin to transfer it from the work surface.

5. Spread the pizza sauce over the crust, then top with the lamb mixture. Scatter over the cheese and bake in the preheated oven for 15–20 minutes, or until the cheese is turning golden and the crust is crisp underneath. Scatter over the remaining pine nuts a little before the end of cooking. Drizzle over the tzatziki and milk mixture and serve immediately.

Makes 1 large pizza

* 1 quantity Basic Pizza Dough

Topping
½ tbsp olive oil
1 onion, finely chopped
2 garlic cloves, crushed
1lb 2 oz/500 g lean ground lamb
2 tbsp tomato paste
2 oz/55 g prepared grilled or roasted eggplant in oil, coarsely chopped
2 tsp dried oregano
3 tbsp pine nuts
scant 1 cup cold water
¾ cup prepared pizza sauce
1⅓ cups roughly chopped feta cheese
salt and pepper
4 tbsp tzatziki, mixed with 1 tbsp milk, to garnish

Chicken & Spinach Pizza

1. Make the pizza dough as described on page 10. Punch down the dough by gently kneading for about a minute, then divide into two balls. To roll out the dough, flatten each ball, then, using a rolling pin, roll out on a lightly floured work surface, giving a quarter turn between each roll.

2. Preheat the oven to 425°F/220°C. Place the pizza crusts on two baking sheets, using a rolling pin to transfer them from the work surface.

3. Place the spinach in a small saucepan over medium heat and cook for 1–2 minutes, until it has wilted. Drain through a strainer and press down with the back of a spoon to remove any excess water.

4. Divide the pizza sauce between the two pizza crusts, spreading almost to the edges. Scatter the spinach, chicken, and red bell pepper over the pizza crusts and top with the cheese. Season to taste with salt and pepper.

5. Bake in the preheated oven for 10–12 minutes, or until the cheese is melting and turning golden and the crusts are crisp underneath. Serve immediately.

Makes 2 pizzas

1 quantity Basic Pizza Dough

Topping
9 oz/250 g fresh spinach, washed and drained

¾ cup prepared pizza sauce

heaping 1 cup coarsely torn cooked chicken strips

1 large prepared roasted red bell pepper, drained and thinly sliced

9 oz/250 g light mozzarella cheese, drained and coarsely torn

salt and pepper

40

Smoked Ham, Mushroom & Ricotta Cheese Pizza

1. Make the pizza dough as described on page 10. Punch down the dough by gently kneading for about a minute, then divide into four balls. To roll out the dough, flatten each ball, then, using a rolling pin, roll out on a lightly floured work surface, giving a quarter turn between each roll.

2. Preheat the oven to 425°F/220°C. Place the pizza crusts on two baking sheets, using a rolling pin to transfer them from the work surface.

3. Divide the pesto among the four pizza crusts, spreading almost to the edges. Scatter over the turkey ham, onion, yellow bell pepper, and mushrooms.

4. Spoon the cheese evenly over the pizzas and season to taste with salt and pepper.

5. Bake in the preheated oven for 15–18 minutes, or until the cheese is turning golden and the crusts are crisp underneath. Serve immediately.

Makes 4 small pizzas

* 1 quantity Basic Pizza Dough

Topping
½ cup prepared red pesto
6 oz/175 g cooked turkey ham, torn into strips
1 small red onion, finely sliced
1 yellow bell pepper, seeded and finely sliced
1¼ cups sliced button mushrooms
1 cup ricotta cheese
salt and pepper

Fish & Seafood

41

Smoked Salmon & Dill Pizza

1. Make the pizza dough as described on page 10. Punch down the dough by gently kneading for about a minute, then divide into two balls. To roll out the dough, flatten each ball, then, using a rolling pin, roll out on a lightly floured work surface, giving a quarter turn between each roll.

2. Preheat the oven to 450°F/230°C. Place the pizza crusts on two baking sheets, using a rolling pin to transfer them from the work surface.

3. Divide the pizza sauce between the two pizza crusts, spreading almost to the edges. Scatter over the salmon and spoon the ricotta in small amounts evenly over the crusts. Drizzle with the dill sauce and season to taste with pepper.

4. Bake in the preheated oven for 10–12 minutes, or until the cheese is turning golden and the crusts are crisp underneath. If the pizzas are browning too quickly, cover with foil for the last few minutes of cooking.

5. Garnish with arugula and serve immediately.

Makes 2 pizzas

* 1 quantity Basic Pizza Dough

Topping
¾ cup prepared pizza sauce

5½ oz/150 g smoked salmon, torn into strips

1 cup ricotta cheese

2 tbsp prepared dill sauce, or 2 tsp fresh dill, finely chopped

pepper

fresh arugula leaves, to garnish

42

Smoked Salmon with Spinach & Capers Pizza

1. Make the pizza dough as described on page 10. Punch down the dough by gently kneading for about a minute, then divide into two balls. To roll out the dough, flatten each ball, then, using a rolling pin, roll out on a lightly floured work surface, giving a quarter turn between each roll.

2. Preheat the oven to 425°F/220°C. Place the pizza crusts on two baking sheets, using a rolling pin to transfer them from the work surface.

3. Place the spinach in a small saucepan over medium heat and cook for 1–2 minutes, until it has wilted. Drain through a strainer and press down with the back of a spoon to remove any excess water.

4. Divide the pizza sauce between the two pizza crusts, spreading almost to the edges. Arrange the spinach, salmon, and capers on the pizzas and top with the cheese.

5. Bake in the preheated oven for 10–12 minutes, or until the cheese is melting and turning golden and the crusts are crisp underneath. Serve immediately.

Makes 2 pizzas

✳ 1 quantity Basic Pizza Dough

Topping
9 oz/250 g fresh spinach, washed and drained

¾ cup prepared pizza sauce

5½ oz/150 g smoked salmon, torn into strips

scant ½ cup drained capers

9 oz/250 g mozzarella cheese, drained and coarsely torn

43

Sushi-Style Smoked Salmon with Wasabi Pizza

1. Make the pizza dough as described on page 10. Punch down the dough by gently kneading for about a minute, then divide into two balls. To roll out the dough, flatten each ball, then, using a rolling pin, roll out on a lightly floured work surface, giving a quarter turn between each roll.

2. Preheat the oven to 425°F/220°C. Place the pizza crusts on two baking sheets, using a rolling pin to transfer them from the work surface.

3. Divide the pizza sauce between the two pizza crusts, spreading almost to the edges. Place the salmon, scallions, and ginger over the pizzas, then spoon small amounts of the cheese evenly over the top.

4. Bake in the preheated oven for 10–12 minutes, or until the cheese is turning golden and the crusts are crisp underneath. If the pizzas are browning too quickly, cover with foil for the last few minutes of cooking.

5. Drizzle the wasabi dressing over the cooked pizzas and serve immediately.

Makes 2 pizzas

1 quantity Basic Pizza Dough

Topping
¾ cup prepared pizza sauce
5½ oz/150 g smoked salmon, torn into strips
6 scallions, finely chopped
1¼ oz/35 g pickled ginger, chopped
1 cup ricotta cheese
2 tsp wasabi sauce, mixed with 1 tbsp vegetable oil, to garnish

Spicy Shrimp Salsa Pizza

1 Make the pizza dough as described on page 10. Punch down the dough by gently kneading for about a minute, then divide into two balls. To roll out the dough, flatten each ball, then, using a rolling pin, roll out on a lightly floured work surface, giving a quarter turn between each roll.

2 Preheat the oven to 425°F/220°C. Place the pizza crusts on two baking sheets, using a rolling pin to transfer them from the work surface.

3 Divide the salsa between the two pizza crusts, spreading almost to the edges. Scatter over the shrimp, yellow bell pepper, scallions, chile flakes, and cheese. Season to taste with salt and pepper.

4 Bake in the preheated oven for 10–12 minutes, or until the cheese is melting and starting to turn golden and the crusts are crisp underneath. Serve immediately.

Makes 2 pizzas

* 1 quantity Basic Pizza Dough

Topping
⅔ cup prepared spicy tomato salsa

5½ oz/150 g cooked jumbo shrimp

1 yellow bell pepper, seeded and finely chopped

6 scallions, chopped

pinch dried chile flakes

1¾ oz/50 g Parmesan cheese, shaved

salt and pepper

Tuna, Fennel &
Red Onion Calzone

① Make the pizza dough as described on page 10. Punch down the dough by gently kneading for about a minute, then divide into two balls. To roll out the dough, flatten each ball, then, using a rolling pin, roll out on a lightly floured work surface, giving a quarter turn between each roll.

② Preheat the oven to 425°F/220°C. Place the pizza crusts on two baking sheets, using a rolling pin to transfer them from the work surface.

③ Divide the pizza sauce between the two pizza crusts, spreading almost to the edges. Scatter over half of the onion, tuna, fennel, and cheese on one-half of each crust.

④ Brush the edges of the crusts with a little water, then fold them over the filling to make two half-moon-shape calzones. Seal the edges all the way around by folding a little of the dough over and pinching the edges together. Make small holes in the top of each calzone with the tip of a knife.

⑤ Bake in the preheated oven for 10–15 minutes, or until the tops are golden and the crusts are crisp underneath. Serve immediately.

Makes 2 calzones

✳ 1 quantity Basic Pizza Dough

Filling
¾ cup prepared pizza sauce
1 small red onion, finely chopped
10½ oz/300 g canned tuna, drained
½ fennel bulb, very finely sliced
1⅓ cups grated cheddar cheese

Tuna, Olive & Ricotta Cheese Pizza

1. Make the pizza dough as described on page 10. Punch down the dough by gently kneading for about a minute, then divide into two balls. To roll out the dough, flatten each ball, then, using a rolling pin, roll out on a lightly floured work surface, giving a quarter turn between each roll.

2. Preheat the oven to 425°F/220°C. Place the pizza crusts on two baking sheets, using a rolling pin to transfer them from the work surface.

3. Divide the pizza sauce between the two pizza crusts, spreading almost to the edges. Scatter over the tuna, tomatoes, olives, and herbs. Spoon small amounts of the cheese evenly over the crusts in small amounts, then drizzle over the reserved oil and season to taste with salt and pepper.

4. Bake in the preheated oven for 10–12 minutes, or until the cheese is melting and turning golden and the crusts are crisp underneath. Garnish with the basil leaves and serve immediately.

Makes 2 pizzas

* 1 quantity Basic Pizza Dough

Topping
¾ cup prepared pizza sauce

10½ oz/300 g canned tuna, drained

1⅓ cups drained and quartered sun-dried tomatoes in oil, reserving 1 tbsp of the oil

½ cup halved, pitted mixed olives

1 tsp dried herbes de provence

1 cup ricotta cheese

salt and pepper

fresh basil leaves, to garnish

Chile Tuna Pizza

1. Make the pizza dough as described on page 10. Punch down the dough by gently kneading for about a minute, then divide into two balls. To roll out the dough, flatten each ball, then, using a rolling pin, roll out on a lightly floured work surface, giving a quarter turn between each roll.

2. Preheat the oven to 425°F/220°C. Place the pizza crusts on two baking sheets, using a rolling pin to transfer them from the work surface.

3. Divide the pizza sauce between the two pizza crusts, spreading almost to the edges. Scatter over the tuna, tomatoes, corn kernels, mushrooms, and chile flakes. Top with the cheese and season to taste with salt and pepper.

4. Bake in the preheated oven for 10–12 minutes, or until the cheese is melting and turning golden and the crusts are crisp underneath. Serve immediately.

Makes 2 pizzas

✳ 1 quantity Basic Pizza Dough

Topping
¾ cup prepared pizza sauce
10½ oz/300 g canned tuna, drained
6 cherry tomatoes, thinly sliced
scant ½ cup drained canned corn kernels
1½ cups thinly sliced button mushrooms
1 tsp dried chile flakes
9 oz/250 g mozzarella cheese, drained and coarsely torn
salt and pepper

Crab, Gruyère Cheese & Spinach Pizza

1. Make the pizza dough as described on page 10. Punch down the dough by gently kneading for about a minute, then divide into two balls. To roll out the dough, flatten each ball, then, using a rolling pin, roll out on a lightly floured work surface, giving a quarter turn between each roll.

2. Preheat the oven to 425°F/220°C. Place the pizza crusts on two baking sheets, using a rolling pin to transfer them from the work surface.

3. Put the spinach in a small saucepan and cook over medium heat for 1–2 minutes, until it has wilted. Drain the spinach through a strainer and press down with the back of a spoon to remove any excess water.

4. Divide the pizza sauce between the two pizza crusts, spreading almost to the edges. Scatter over the spinach, crabmeat, red bell peppers, and cheese and season to taste with salt and pepper.

5. Bake in the preheated oven for 10–12 minutes, or until the cheese is melting and turning golden and the crusts are crisp underneath. Serve immediately.

Makes 2 pizzas

* 1 quantity Basic Pizza Dough

Topping
9 oz/250 g fresh spinach, washed and drained

¾ cup prepared pizza sauce

6 oz/175 g cooked white crabmeat

2 prepared roasted red bell peppers, drained and finely sliced

1⅔ cups grated Gruyère cheese

salt and pepper

Crab, Asparagus & Ricotta Cheese Pizza

1. Make the pizza dough as described on page 10. Punch down the dough by gently kneading for about a minute, then divide into four balls. To roll out the dough, flatten each ball, then, using a rolling pin, roll out on a lightly floured work surface, giving a quarter turn between each roll.

2. Preheat the oven to 425°F/220°C. Place the pizza crusts on two baking sheets, using a rolling pin to transfer them from the work surface.

3. Bring a small saucepan of lightly salted water to a boil, then add the asparagus spears and cook for 2–3 minutes. Drain and plunge into ice cold water for 1–2 minutes (to retain the bright green color). Drain well and chop coarsely.

4. Divide the pizza sauce between the four pizza crusts, spreading almost to the edges. Scatter over the cooked asparagus, crabmeat, and onion. Top with the cheese and drizzle over the oil. Season to taste with salt and pepper.

5. Bake in the preheated oven for 10–12 minutes, or until the cheese is melting and turning golden and the crusts are crisp underneath. Serve immediately.

Makes 4 small pizzas

* 1 quantity Basic Pizza Dough

Topping
5½ oz/150 g asparagus spears, trimmed
¾ cup prepared pizza sauce
6 oz/175 g cooked white crabmeat
1 red onion, finely sliced
1 cup ricotta cheese
1 tbsp extra virgin olive oil
salt and pepper

Monkfish & Bacon Pizza

1. Make the pizza dough as described on page 10. Punch down the dough by gently kneading for about a minute, then divide into two balls. To roll out the dough, flatten each ball, then, using a rolling pin, roll out on a lightly floured work surface, giving a quarter turn between each roll.

2. Preheat the oven to 425°F/220°C. Place the pizza crusts on two baking sheets, using a rolling pin to transfer them from the work surface.

3. Place the monkfish on a small baking sheet, drizzle with the oil, and season to taste with salt and pepper. Roast in the preheated oven for 18–20 minutes, or until the fish is just cooked and the flesh is opaque. Remove from the oven and flake into chunky pieces.

4. Heat a nonstick skillet over high heat, add the bacon, and dry-fry for 2–3 minutes, or until starting to turn crispy. Remove from the skillet and drain on paper towels.

5. Divide the pizza sauce between the two pizza crusts, spreading almost to the edges. Scatter over the fish and bacon, then add the red bell pepper and finish with the cheese. Season to taste with salt and pepper.

6. Bake in the preheated oven for 8–10 minutes, or until the cheese is melting and golden and the crusts are crisp underneath. Serve immediately.

Makes 2 pizzas

* 1 quantity Basic Pizza Dough

Topping

9 oz/250 g fresh monkfish fillet

1 tbsp lemon olive oil

4½ oz/125 g Canadian bacon or smoked bacon, cut into small dice

¾ cup prepared pizza sauce

1 prepared roasted red bell pepper, drained and finely sliced

scant 1 cup grated sharp cheddar cheese

salt and pepper

51

Chili Crab with Mussels Pizza

1. Make the pizza dough as described on page 10. Punch down the dough by gently kneading for about a minute, then divide into two balls. To roll out the dough, flatten each ball, then, using a rolling pin, roll out on a lightly floured work surface, giving a quarter turn between each roll.

2. Preheat the oven to 425°F/220°C. Place the pizza crusts on two baking sheets, using a rolling pin to transfer them from the work surface.

3. Divide the salsa sauce between the two pizza crusts, spreading almost to the edges. Scatter over the crab, mussels, and scallions, then drizzle the sweet chili sauce evenly over the pizzas. Top with the cheese and season to taste with salt and pepper.

4. Bake in the preheated oven for 10–12 minutes, or until the cheese is melting and turning golden and the crusts are crisp underneath. Serve immediately.

Makes 2 pizzas

1 quantity Basic Pizza Dough

Topping
¾ cup prepared tomato salsa

6 oz/175 g cooked white crabmeat

5½ oz/150 g cooked mussels, shelled

½ bunch scallions, chopped

4 tbsp sweet chili sauce

1⅓ cups grated mild cheddar cheese

salt and pepper

Seafood Pizza

1. Make the pizza dough as described on page 10, adding the rosemary with the flour. Punch down the dough by gently kneading for about a minute, then divide into two balls. To roll out the dough, flatten each ball, then, using a rolling pin, roll out on a lightly floured work surface, giving a quarter turn between each roll.

2. Preheat the oven to 425°F/220°C. Place the pizza crusts on two baking sheets, using a rolling pin to transfer them from the work surface.

3. Divide the pizza sauce between the two pizza crusts, spreading almost to the edges. Scatter over the seafood and onion and top with the mozzarella cheese and Parmesan cheese. Season to taste with salt and pepper.

4. Bake in the preheated oven for 10–12 minutes, or until the cheeses are melting and golden and the crusts are crisp underneath. Serve immediately.

Makes 2 pizzas

1 quantity Basic Pizza Dough

1 tsp dried rosemary

Topping

¾ cup prepared pizza sauce

7 oz/200 g mixed cooked seafood, such as shrimp, mussels, and squid rings, drained well on paper towels

1 red onion, finely chopped

3 oz/85 g mozzarella cheese, drained and coarsely torn

3 oz/85 g Parmesan cheese, shaved

salt and pepper

Marinara Calzone

1. Make the pizza dough as described on page 10. Punch down the dough by gently kneading for about a minute, then divide into four balls. To roll out the dough, flatten each ball, then, using a rolling pin, roll out on a lightly floured work surface, giving a quarter turn between each roll. Roll each one into a circle with a diameter of about 7½ inches/19 cm.

2. Preheat the oven to 425°F/220°C. Place the pizza crusts on two baking sheets, using a rolling pin to transfer them from the work surface.

3. Divide the pizza sauce among the four pizza crusts, spreading almost to the edges. Scatter over the seafood and basil on half of each crust and top with the cheese. Season to taste with salt and pepper.

4. Brush the edges of the crusts with a little water, then fold them over the filling to make four half-moon-shape calzones. Seal the edges all the way around by folding a little of the dough over and pinching the edges together. Make some small holes in the top of each calzone with the tip of a sharp knife.

5. Bake in the preheated oven for 10–15 minutes, or until the tops are golden and the crusts are crisp underneath. Serve immediately.

Makes 4 individual calzones

1 quantity Basic Pizza Dough

Filling

¾ cup prepared pizza sauce

7 oz/200 g mixed cooked seafood, such as shrimp, mussels, and squid rings, drained well on paper towels

2 tbsp finely chopped fresh basil

7 oz/200 g mozzarella cheese, drained and coarsely torn

salt and pepper

54

Tilapia with Sharp Cheddar & Red Onion Pizza

1. Make the pizza dough as described on page 10. Punch down the dough by gently kneading for about a minute, then divide into two balls. To roll out the dough, flatten each ball, then, using a rolling pin, roll out on a lightly floured work surface, giving a quarter turn between each roll.

2. Preheat the oven to 400°F/200°C. Place the pizza crusts on two baking sheets, using a rolling pin to transfer them from the work surface.

3. Place the tilapia fillet on a small baking sheet, drizzle with the oil, and season to taste with salt and pepper. Roast in the preheated oven for 10–12 minutes, until just cooked and the flesh is opaque. Remove from the oven and flake into chunky pieces.

4. Increase the oven temperature to 425°F/220°C. Divide the pizza sauce between the two pizza crusts, spreading almost to the edges. Scatter the tilapia over the pizzas, then add the onion and the cheese. Season to taste with salt and pepper.

5. Bake in the preheated oven for 8–10 minutes, or until the cheese is melting and turning golden and the crusts are crisp underneath. Serve immediately.

Makes 2 pizzas

※ 1 quantity Basic Pizza Dough

Topping
7 oz/200 g tilapia fillet
½ tbsp olive oil
¾ cup prepared pizza sauce
1 red onion, finely sliced
1¾ cups grated sharp cheddar cheese
salt and pepper

Mussel & Caramelized Fennel Pizza

1. Make the pizza dough as described on page 10. Punch down the dough by gently kneading for about a minute, then divide into two balls. To roll out the dough, flatten each ball, then, using a rolling pin, roll out on a lightly floured work surface, giving a quarter turn between each roll.

2. Preheat the oven to 400°F/200°C. Place the pizza crusts on two baking sheets, using a rolling pin to transfer them from the work surface.

3. Heat half of the oil in a ridged grill pan over medium heat. Add the fennel and garlic and cook over medium–high heat for 4–5 minutes, turning regularly until turning golden and starting to char and soften. Remove from the pan and drain on paper towels. Add the remaining oil to the pan and heat, then add the onion and cook for 3–4 minutes, until starting to caramelize. Remove from the pan and drain on paper towels.

4. Divide the pizza sauce between the two pizza crusts, spreading almost to the edges. Scatter over the fennel and onion, add the mussels and chile flakes, and finish with the mozzarella cheese and Parmesan cheese. Season to taste with salt and pepper.

5. Bake in the preheated oven for 10–12 minutes, or until the cheeses are melting and golden and the crusts are crisp underneath. Serve immediately.

Makes 2 pizzas

1 quantity Basic Pizza Dough

Topping
1½ tbsp olive oil
½ fennel bulb, thinly cut into whole slices
2 garlic cloves, crushed
1 red onion, sliced into rings
¾ cup prepared pizza sauce
7 oz/200 g cooked mussels, shelled
pinch of chile flakes
6 oz/175 g mozzarella cheese, drained and coarsely torn
1 oz/25 g Parmesan cheese, shaved
salt and pepper

Hawaiian Shrimp Pizza

1. Make the pizza dough as described on page 10. Punch down the dough by gently kneading for about a minute, then divide into two balls. To roll out the dough, flatten each ball, then, using a rolling pin, roll out on a lightly floured work surface, giving a quarter turn between each roll.

2. Preheat the oven to 425°F/220°C. Place the pizza crusts on two baking sheets, using a rolling pin to transfer them from the work surface.

3. Divide the salsa between the two pizza crusts, spreading almost to the edges. Scatter over the shrimp, pineapple, and red bell pepper, then top with the cheese.

4. Bake in the preheated oven for 10–12 minutes, or until the cheese is melting and turning golden and the crusts are crisp underneath. Garnish with the chopped cilantro and serve immediately.

Makes 2 pizzas

* 1 quantity Basic Pizza Dough

Topping
¾ cup prepared tomato salsa

7 oz/200 g cooked jumbo shrimp

⅔ cup small fresh pineapple chunks

1 red bell pepper, seeded and finely sliced

9 oz/250 g mozzarella cheese, drained and coarsely torn

fresh chopped cilantro leaves, to garnish

Garlic, Shrimp & Mushroom Calzone

1. Make the pizza dough as described on page 10. Punch down the dough by gently kneading for about a minute, then divide into two balls. To roll out the dough, flatten each ball, then, using a rolling pin, roll out on a lightly floured work surface, giving a quarter turn between each roll.

2. Preheat the oven to 425°F/220°C. Place the pizza crusts on two baking sheets, using a rolling pin to transfer them from the work surface.

3. Heat the oil in a skillet over medium heat. Add the garlic and mushrooms and gently sauté for 2–3 minutes. Add the shrimp and cook for 1–2 minutes, until they have turned pink and are just cooked. Season to taste with salt and pepper, remove from the skillet and drain on paper towels.

4. Spread the pizza sauce over the two pizza crusts, then scatter over the mushroom-and-shrimp mixture on one-half of each of the crusts. Add the corn kernels and top with the cheese.

5. Brush the edges of the crusts with a little water, then fold them over the filling to make two half-moon-shape calzones. Seal the edges by folding over a little of the dough and pinching the edges together. Make small holes in the top of each calzone with the tip of a knife.

6. Bake in the preheated oven for 10–15 minutes, or until the tops are golden and the crusts are crisp underneath. Serve immediately.

Makes 2 calzone

* 1 quantity Basic Pizza Dough

Filling

1 tbsp olive oil

1 garlic clove, crushed

7 oz/200 g button mushrooms

7 oz/200 g shrimp, peeled and deveined

¾ cup prepared pizza sauce

scant ½ cup drained canned corn kernels

9 oz/250 g mozzarella cheese, drained and coarsely torn

salt and pepper

Clam & Green Pepper Pizza

1. Make the pizza dough as described on page 10. Punch down the dough by gently kneading for about a minute, then divide into two balls. To roll out the dough, flatten each ball, then, using a rolling pin, roll out on a lightly floured work surface, giving a quarter turn between each roll.

2. Preheat the oven to 425°F/220°C. Place the pizza crusts on two baking sheets, using a rolling pin to transfer them from the work surface.

3. Divide the tomato salsa between the two pizza crusts, spreading almost to the edges. Scatter over the clams, green bell pepper, onion, and oregano and top with the mozzarella cheese and Parmesan cheese. Season to taste with salt and pepper.

4. Bake in the preheated oven for 8–10 minutes, or until the cheeses are melting and turning golden and the crusts are crisp underneath. Serve immediately.

Makes 2 pizzas

* 1 quantity Basic Pizza Dough

Topping
¾ cup prepared tomato salsa

10 oz/280 g canned baby clams, drained

1 green bell pepper, seeded and finely sliced

1 red onion, finely sliced

1 tsp dried oregano

4½ oz/125 g mozzarella cheese, drained and coarsely torn

1¾ oz/50 g Parmesan cheese, shaved

salt and pepper

59

Jumbo Shrimp & Cilantro Pesto Pizza

1. Make the pizza dough as described on page 10, adding the chile flakes with the flour. Punch down the dough by gently kneading for about a minute, then divide into two balls. To roll out the dough, flatten each ball, then, using a rolling pin, roll out on a lightly floured work surface, giving a quarter turn between each roll.

2. Preheat the oven to 425°F/220°C. Place the pizza crusts on two baking sheets, using a rolling pin to transfer them from the work surface.

3. Divide the cilantro pesto between the two pizza crusts, spreading almost to the edges. Scatter over the scallions, shrimp, and cheese, then season to taste with salt and pepper.

4. Bake in the preheated oven for 10–12 minutes, or until the cheese is melted and turning golden and the crusts are crisp underneath. Serve immediately.

Makes 2 pizzas

* 1 quantity Basic Pizza Dough
1 tsp dried chile flakes

Topping
½ cup prepared cilantro pesto
8 scallions, finely chopped
10½ oz/300 g cooked jumbo shrimp
4½ oz/125 g Parmesan cheese, shaved
salt and pepper

60

Scallop, Pea, Leek & Lemon Pizza

1. Make the pizza dough as described on page 10. Punch down the dough by gently kneading for about a minute, then divide into two balls. To roll out the dough, flatten each ball, then, using a rolling pin, roll out on a lightly floured work surface, giving a quarter turn between each roll.

2. Preheat the oven to 425°F/220°C. Place the pizza crusts on two baking sheets, using a rolling pin to transfer them from the work surface.

3. Heat the oil in a small skillet over medium–high heat. Add the scallops and sauté for 5–7 minutes, turning occasionally, until they are starting to brown and are just cooked. Remove from the skillet and drain on paper towels.

4. Divide the pizza sauce between the two pizza crusts, spreading almost to the edges. Scatter over the leek, peas, and scallops. Top with the cheese and season to taste with salt and pepper.

5. Bake in the preheated oven for 15–18 minutes, or until the cheese is melting and turning golden and the crusts are crisp underneath. Garnish with the lemon zest and serve immediately.

Makes 2 pizzas

1 quantity Basic Pizza Dough

Topping
1 tbsp olive oil
7 oz/200 g roeless scallops
¾ cup prepared pizza sauce
1 small leek, finely chopped
⅔ cup frozen peas, thawed and drained on paper towels
7 oz/200 g light mozzarella cheese, drained and coarsely torn
salt and pepper
finely grated zest of 1 lemon, to garnish

Nice &
Spicy

61

Triple Chile Pizza

1. Make the pizza dough as described on page 10, adding the chile flakes with the flour. Punch down the dough by gently kneading for about a minute, then divide into two balls. To roll out the dough, flatten each ball, then, using a rolling pin, roll out on a lightly floured work surface, giving a quarter turn between each roll.

2. Preheat the broiler to high, place the steak on a broiler rack, and cook for 10–12 minutes, turning once, or until cooked to your liking. Remove from the broiler, let rest for 5 minutes, then slice thinly.

3. Preheat the oven to 425°F/220°C. Place the pizza crusts on two baking sheets, using a roiling pin to transfer them from the work surface.

4. Spread the salsa over the pizza crusts, spreading almost to the edges. Top with the steak, jalapeño peppers, and red bell pepper. Drizzle the chipotle paste evenly over the pizzas, top with the cheese, and season to taste with salt and pepper.

5. Bake in the preheated oven for 15–20 minutes, or until the cheese is melting and turning golden and the crusts are crisp underneath. Serve immediately.

Makes 2 pizzas

1 quantity Basic Pizza Dough
1 tsp dried chile flakes

Topping
12 oz/350 g sirloin or top round steak, trimmed
¾ cup prepared tomato salsa
2 tbsp drained, sliced hot red jalapeño peppers in oil
2 prepared roasted red bell peppers, drained and finely sliced
1 tbsp chipotle paste
1½ cups grated cheddar or Monterey Jack cheese
salt and pepper

62

Spicy Bell Peppers & Goat Cheese Pizza

1. Make the pizza dough as described on page 10. Punch down the dough by gently kneading for about a minute, then divide into two balls. To roll out the dough, flatten each ball, then, using a rolling pin, roll out on a lightly floured work surface, giving a quarter turn between each roll.

2. Preheat the oven to 400°F/200°C. Place the pizza crusts on two baking sheets, using a rolling pin to transfer them from the work surface.

3. Place the onion, red bell pepper, yellow bell pepper, chiles, and garlic on a baking sheet, drizzle over the oil, season to taste with salt and pepper, and toss well to coat. Place in the preheated oven and cook for 20–25 minutes, until softened and starting to char around the edges.

4. Divide the pizza sauce between the two pizza crusts, spreading almost to the edges. Scatter over the roasted vegetables and top with the cheese.

5. Bake in the preheated oven for 10–12 minutes, or until the cheese is melting and turning golden and the crusts are crisp underneath. Serve immediately.

Makes 2 pizzas

* 1 quantity Basic Pizza Dough

Topping
1 onion, thinly sliced

1 red bell pepper, seeded and finely sliced

1 yellow bell pepper, seeded and finely sliced

2 red chiles, seeded and roughly chopped

2 garlic cloves, crushed

1 tbsp extra virgin olive oil

¾ cup prepared pizza sauce

7 oz/200 g soft goat cheese, thinly sliced

salt and pepper

Tapenade & Mozzarella Pizza

1. Make the pizza dough as described on page 10. Punch down the dough by gently kneading for about a minute, then divide into two balls. To roll out the dough, flatten each ball, then, using a rolling pin, roll out on a lightly floured work surface, giving a quarter turn between each roll.

2. Preheat the oven to 425°F/220°C. Place the pizza crusts on two baking sheets, using a rolling pin to transfer them from the work surface.

3. Divide the tapenade between the two pizza crusts, spreading almost to the edges. Scatter over the onion, tomatoes, chiles, oregano, and cheese. Season to taste with salt and pepper.

4. Bake in the preheated oven for 8–10 minutes, or until the cheese is melting and turning golden and the crusts are crispy underneath. Serve immediately.

Makes 2 pizzas

1 quantity Basic Pizza Dough

Topping

6 tbsp prepared black olive tapenade

1 small red onion, finely chopped

6 cherry tomatoes, finely sliced

2 red chiles, seeded and finely chopped

2 tsp finely chopped fresh oregano

9 oz/250 g mozzarella cheese, drained and roughly torn

salt and pepper

Indian-Style Pizza

1. Make the pizza dough as described on page 10. Punch down the dough by gently kneading for about a minute, then divide into two balls. To roll out the dough, flatten each ball, then, using a rolling pin, roll out on a lightly floured work surface, giving a quarter turn between each roll.

2. Preheat the oven to 425°F/220°C. Place the pizza crusts on two baking sheets, using a rolling pin to transfer them from the work surface.

3. Divide the pesto between the two pizza crusts, spreading almost to the edges. Scatter over the chicken and scallions, then drizzle over the chili sauce and top with the cheese. Season to taste with salt and pepper.

4. Bake in the preheated oven for 10–12 minutes, or until the cheese is melting and turning golden and the crusts are crisp underneath. Garnish with the fresh cilantro and serve immediately.

Makes 2 pizzas

* 1 quantity Basic Pizza Dough

Topping

½ cup prepared cilantro pesto

heaping 2 cups cooked roughly chopped Indian spiced chicken pieces

1 bunch scallions, finely chopped

3 tbsp sweet chili sauce

1⅓ cups grated mild cheddar cheese

salt and pepper

fresh cilantro, finely chopped, to garnish

65

Spanish Spicy Pizza

1. Make the pizza dough as described on page 10, adding the paprika with the flour. Punch down the dough by gently kneading for about a minute, then divide into two balls. To roll out the dough, flatten each ball, then, using a rolling pin, roll out on a lightly floured work surface, giving a quarter turn between each roll.

2. Preheat the oven to 425°F/220°C. Place the pizza crusts on two baking sheets, using a rolling pin to transfer them from the work surface.

3. Divide the pizza sauce between the two pizza crusts, spreading almost to the edges. Scatter over the prosciutto, chorizo, and olives and top with the cheese. Season to taste with pepper.

4. Bake in the preheated oven for 10–12 minutes, or until the cheese is melting and golden and the crusts are crisp underneath. Serve immediately.

Makes 2 pizzas

* 1 quantity Basic Pizza Dough
1 tsp smoked paprika

Topping
¾ cup prepared pizza sauce

3½ oz/100 g prosciutto, roughly torn

1¾ oz/50 g spicy chorizo sausage, thinly sliced

½ cup halved mixed Spanish anchovy- or chile-stuffed olives in garlic oil

9 oz/250 g mozzarella cheese, drained and roughly torn

pepper

Spicy Chicken Pizza

1. Make the pizza dough as described on page 10. Punch down the dough by gently kneading for about a minute, then divide into two balls. To roll out the dough, flatten each ball, then, using a rolling pin, roll out on a lightly floured work surface, giving a quarter turn between each roll.

2. Place the pizza crusts on two baking sheets, using a rolling pin to transfer them from the work surface.

3. Place the oil in a dish and add the chicken, spices, oregano, and honey. Cover and let marinate in the refrigerator for 1–2 hours.

4. Preheat the oven to 425°F/220°C. Place the strips of cheese around the rim of each pizza, about ¾ inch/2 cm from the edges. Use a pastry brush to wet the edges, then fold over to seal the cheese inside the crust.

5. Place the marinated chicken on a baking sheet and bake in the preheated oven for 15–20 minutes, until just cooked through.

6. Divide the pizza sauce between the two pizza crusts, spreading almost to the edges. Scatter over the chicken, onion, yellow bell pepper, and cheese. Season to taste with salt and pepper.

7. Bake in the preheated oven for 12–15 minutes, or until the cheese is melting and turning golden and the crusts are crisp underneath. Drizzle with the sour cream and serve immediately.

Makes 2 pizzas

* 1 quantity Basic Pizza Dough
3½ oz/100 g mozzarella cheese, drained and cut into short strips

Topping
1 tbsp vegetable oil
14 oz/400 g skinless, boneless chicken breast, cut into small cubes
1 tsp garlic pepper
1½ tsp paprika
1 tsp ground ginger
½ tsp cayenne pepper
1 tsp dried oregano
1 tbsp honey
¾ cup prepared pizza sauce
1 red onion, finely sliced
1 yellow bell pepper, seeded and finely sliced
9 oz/250 g mozzarella cheese, drained and roughly torn
salt and pepper
4 tbsp sour cream, to serve

Chili con Carne Calzone

1. Make the pizza dough as described on page 10. Punch down the dough by gently kneading for about a minute, then divide into four balls. To roll out the dough, flatten each ball, then, using a rolling pin, roll out on a lightly floured work surface to a diameter of about 19 cm/7½ inches, giving a quarter turn between each roll.

2. Preheat the oven to 425°F/220°C. Place the pizza crusts on two baking sheets, using a rolling pin to transfer them from the work surface.

3. Heat the oil in a saucepan over medium heat, add the onion and garlic, and sauté for 3-4 minutes. Add the beef and spices and cook for 4-5 minutes. Stir in the tomato paste, tomatoes, water, and beans and season to taste with salt and pepper. Cook for 15-20 minutes, or until the beef is cooked and the sauce is thick.

4. Brush the edges of each pizza crust with a little water and divide the chili between them. Fold over the crusts to make four half-moon-shape calzones. Seal the edges by folding over a little of the dough and pinching the edges together. Make small holes in the top of each calzone with the tip of a knife.

5. Bake in the preheated oven for 10–15 minutes, or until the tops are golden and the crusts are crisp underneath. Serve immediately.

Makes 4 small calzones

* 1 quantity Basic Pizza Dough

Filling
1 tbsp vegetable oil
1 onion, finely chopped
1 garlic clove, crushed
9 oz/250 g lean ground beef
1 tbsp chili powder
1 tsp ground coriander
1 tbsp tomato paste
scant 1 cup canned chopped tomatoes
scant ½ cup cold water
½ cup drained and rinsed canned kidney beans
salt and pepper

68

Cajun-Spiced Chicken Pizza

1. Make the pizza dough as described on page 10, adding the oregano with the flour. Punch down the dough by gently kneading for about a minute, then divide into two balls. To roll out the dough, flatten each ball, then, using a rolling pin, roll out on a lightly floured work surface, giving a quarter turn between each roll.

2. Place the pizza crusts on two baking sheets, using a rolling pin to transfer them from the work surface.

3. Mix half of the oil with the spices, garlic, and oregano. Add the chicken and stir to coat well. Cover and let marinate in the refrigerator for at least 1–2 hours.

4. Preheat the oven to 425°F/220°C. Heat the remaining oil in a nonstick skillet over medium heat, then add the chicken and cook for 5–6 minutes, stirring regularly, until just cooked.

5. Divide the pizza sauce between the two pizza crusts, spreading almost to the edges. Scatter over the chicken, onion, and yellow bell pepper. Top with the cheese and season to taste with salt and pepper.

6. Bake in the preheated oven for 10–12 minutes, or until the cheese is melting and turning golden and the crusts are crisp underneath. Serve immediately.

Makes 2 pizzas

1 quantity Basic Pizza Dough
2 tsp dried oregano

Topping
2 tbsp olive oil
1 tbsp paprika
½ tsp cayenne pepper
1 garlic clove, crushed
2 tsp dried oregano
14 oz/400 g skinless, boneless chicken breast, cut into small strips
¾ cup prepared pizza sauce
1 red onion, finely sliced
1 yellow bell pepper, seeded and finely sliced
9 oz/250 g mozzarella cheese, drained and roughly torn
salt and pepper

Pizza Mexicana

① Make the pizza dough as described on page 10. Punch down the dough by gently kneading for about a minute. Using a rolling pin, roll out the dough to a 15 x 10½-inch/ 38 x 26-cm rectangle on a lightly floured work surface.

② Heat the oil in a medium saucepan over medium heat. Add the onion and garlic and gently sauté for 3–4 minutes, until starting to soften. Add the chiles and red bell pepper and cook for an additional 1–2 minutes, then add the beef and cook over medium–high heat for 4-5 minutes, until lightly browned all over.

③ Add the tomato paste and cook for 1 minute, stirring continuously. Stir in the water and beans and season to taste with salt and pepper. Cover and simmer for 15–20 minutes, stirring occasionally, until the meat is thoroughly cooked and the sauce is spreadable. Remove from the heat and let cool.

④ Preheat the oven to 425°F/220°C. Place the pizza crust on a 15 x 10½-inch/38 x 26-cm rectangular baking sheet, using a rolling pin to transfer it from the work surface.

⑤ Spread the salsa over the pizza crust, then top with the beef mixture. Scatter over the jalapeño peppers and cheese and bake in the oven for 15–20 minutes, or until the cheese is melting and turning golden and the crust is crisp underneath. Garnish with the guacamole and fresh cilantro and serve immediately.

Makes 1 large pizza

1 quantity Basic Pizza Dough

Topping

1 tbsp vegetable oil

1 onion, finely chopped

2 garlic cloves, crushed

2 red chiles, seeded and finely chopped

1 red bell pepper, seeded and chopped

14 oz/400 g lean ground beef

2 tbsp tomato paste

scant 1 cup cold water

1 cup drained and rinsed canned black beans

¾ cup prepared spicy salsa

⅓ cup drained, sliced hot red jalapeño peppers in oil

1¾ cups grated cheddar cheese

salt and pepper

4 tbsp each of prepared guacamole and fresh chopped cilantro, to garnish

70

Chorizo, Artichoke & Olive Pizza

1. Make the pizza dough as described on page 10. Punch down the dough by gently kneading for about a minute, then divide into two balls. To roll out the dough, flatten each ball, then, using a rolling pin, roll out on a lightly floured work surface, giving a quarter turn between each roll.

2. Preheat the oven to 425°F/220°C. Place the pizza crusts on two baking sheets, using a rolling pin to transfer them from the work surface.

3. Divide the pizza sauce between the two pizza crusts, spreading almost to the edges. Scatter over the chorizo, artichoke hearts, and olives and top with the Manchego cheese and mozzarella cheese. Season to taste with pepper.

4. Bake in the preheated oven for 10–12 minutes, or until the cheeses are melting and turning golden and the crusts are crisp underneath. Cover with foil for the last few minutes of cooking if the chorizo starts to brown too quickly. Serve immediately.

Makes 2 pizzas

1 quantity Basic Pizza Dough

Topping

¾ cup prepared pizza sauce

6 oz/175 g spicy chorizo sausage, thinly sliced

5½ oz/150 g artichoke hearts in vegetable oil, drained and sliced into quarters

½ cup drained and halved Spanish anchovy- or chile-stuffed olives in garlic oil

heaping ¾ cup grated Manchego cheese

3½ oz/100 g mozzarella cheese, drained and roughly torn

pepper

71

Pork Meatball Pizza

1. Make the pizza dough as described on page 10. Punch down the dough by gently kneading for about a minute. Using a rolling pin, roll out the dough to a 15 x 10½-inch/ 38 x 26-cm rectangle on a lightly floured work surface.

2. Heat 1 tablespoon of the oil in a skillet over medium heat. Add the onion and garlic and sauté for 3–4 minutes. Let cool slightly, then mix with the pork, sage, and chile. Season to taste with salt and pepper.

3. Form the mixture into small balls about the size of walnuts. Heat the remaining oil in a skillet over medium–high heat, add the meatballs, and sauté for about 10 minutes, turning regularly until cooked through.

4. Preheat the oven to 425°F/220°C. Place the pizza crust on a 15 x 10½-inch/38 x 26-cm rectangular baking sheet, using a rolling pin to transfer it from the work surface.

5. Spread the pizza sauce over the crust, spreading almost to the edges. Top with the pork, green bell pepper and cheese, then season to taste with salt and pepper.

6. Bake in the oven for 15–20 minutes, or until the cheese is melting and turning golden and the crust is crisp underneath. Serve immediately.

Makes 1 large pizza

1 quantity Basic Pizza Dough

Topping
3 tbsp vegetable oil
1 onion, finely grated
2 garlic cloves, crushed
1lb 2 oz/500 g ground pork
1 tbsp dried sage
1 red chile, seeded and finely chopped
¾ cup prepared pizza sauce
1 green bell pepper, seeded and finely chopped
1¾ cups grated cheddar cheese
salt and pepper

Chile Shrimp Pizza

1. Make the pizza dough as described on page 10. Punch down the dough by gently kneading for about a minute, then divide into two balls. To roll out the dough, flatten each ball, then, using a rolling pin, roll out on a lightly floured work surface, giving a quarter turn between each roll.

2. Preheat the oven to 425°F/220°C. Place the pizza crusts on two baking sheets, using a rolling pin to transfer them from the work surface.

3. Divide the pizza sauce between the two pizza crusts, spreading almost to the edges. Scatter over the shrimp and scallions, drizzle over the harissa paste, and top with the cheese. Season to taste with salt and pepper.

4. Bake in the preheated oven for 10–12 minutes, or until the cheese is melting and turning golden and the crusts are crisp underneath. Garnish with the fresh cilantro and serve immediately.

Makes 2 pizzas

* 1 quantity Basic Pizza Dough

Topping
¾ cup prepared pizza sauce
7 oz/200 g cooked, peeled shrimp
½ bunch scallions, finely chopped
1 tbsp harissa paste mixed with 1 tbsp olive oil
9 oz/250 g mozzarella cheese, drained and roughly torn
salt and pepper
fresh cilantro, roughly chopped, to garnish

Hot Dog & Mustard Pizza

1. Make the pizza dough as described on page 10. Punch down the dough by gently kneading for about a minute. Using a rolling pin, roll out the dough to a 15 x 10½-inch/38 x 26-cm rectangle on a lightly floured work surface.

2. Preheat the oven to 425°F/220°C. Place the pizza crust on a 15 x 10½-inch/38 x 26-cm rectangular baking sheet, using a rolling pin to transfer it from the work surface.

3. Heat the oil in a skillet over medium heat, add the onions, and cook for 10-15 minutes, until colored and softened.

4. Spread the pizza sauce over the crust, then top with the frankfurter pieces, onions, and cheese. Season to taste with salt and pepper.

5. Bake in the oven for 15–20 minutes, or until the cheese is melting and golden and the crust is crisp underneath. Drizzle with mustard and serve immediately.

Makes 1 large pizza

※ 1 quantity Basic Pizza Dough

Topping
1 tbsp vegetable oil
2 large onions, finely sliced
¾ cup prepared pizza sauce
6 frankfurters, chopped into bite-size pieces
1¾ cups grated cheddar cheese
salt and pepper
prepared mustard, to serve

74

Fajita-Style Chicken Pizza

1. Make the pizza dough as described on page 10, adding the paprika with the flour. Punch down the dough by gently kneading for about a minute, then divide into two balls. To roll out the dough, flatten each ball, then, using a rolling pin, roll out on a lightly floured work surface, giving a quarter turn between each roll.

2. Preheat the oven to 425°F/220°C. Place the pizza crusts on two baking sheets, using a rolling pin to transfer them from the work surface.

3. Heat half of the oil in a skillet over medium heat. Add the spices and chicken and sauté for 4–5 minutes, stirring, until just cooked. Remove from the skillet and set aside, then add the remaining oil to the skillet. Add the onion, red and orange bell peppers and sauté for 4–5 minutes, stirring regularly, until softened.

4. Divide the pizza sauce between the two pizza crusts, spreading almost to the edges. Scatter over the chicken and vegetables, top with the cheese, and season to taste with salt and pepper.

5. Bake in the preheated oven for 8–10 minutes, until the cheese is melting and turning golden and the crusts are crisp underneath. Garnish with cilantro and serve immediately with the guacamole and sour cream.

Makes 2 pizzas

* 1 quantity Basic Pizza Dough
1 tsp smoked paprika

Topping

2 tbsp vegetable oil

1 oz/25 g envelope dry fajita spices

14 oz/400 g skinless, boneless chicken breast, cut into small cubes

1 red onion, finely sliced

1 red bell pepper, seeded and finely sliced

1 orange bell pepper, seeded and finely sliced

¾ cup prepared pizza sauce

1¾ cups grated cheddar cheese

salt and pepper

fresh cilantro, to garnish

guacamole and sour cream, to serve

Peppered Steak Pizza

1. Make the pizza dough as described on page 10. Punch down the dough by gently kneading for about a minute, then divide into two balls. To roll out the dough, flatten each ball, then, using a rolling pin, roll out on a lightly floured work surface, giving a quarter turn between each roll.

2. Preheat the oven to 425°F/220°C. Place the pizza crusts on two baking sheets, using a rolling pin to transfer them from the work surface.

3. Press the peppercorns onto both sides of the steak. Add the oil to a skillet and heat over high heat. Add the steak and cook for 5–6 minutes on each side, or until cooked to your liking. Remove from the skillet and let rest for 5 minutes, then slice thinly.

4. Divide the pizza sauce between the two pizza crusts, spreading almost to the edges. Top with the onion, steak, and cheese. Season to taste with salt.

5. Bake in the preheated oven for 10–12 minutes, or until the cheese is melting and turning golden and the crusts are crisp underneath. Garnish with the sour cream drizzle and serve immediately with the arugula.

Makes 2 pizzas

* 1 quantity Basic Pizza Dough

Topping
2 tbsp crushed black peppercorns

12 oz/350 g sirloin or top round steak, trimmed

1 tbsp olive oil

¾ cup prepared pizza sauce

1 red onion, finely sliced

1¾ cups grated sharp cheddar cheese

salt

4 tbsp sour cream mixed with 2 tbsp olive oil, to garnish

fresh arugula leaves, to serve

Pepperoni Pizza

1. Make the pizza dough as described on page 10, adding the chile flakes with the flour. Punch down the dough by gently kneading for about a minute, then divide into two balls. To roll out the dough, flatten each ball, then, using a rolling pin, roll out on a lightly floured work surface, giving a quarter turn between each roll.

2. Preheat the oven to 425°F/220°C. Place the pizza crusts on two baking sheets, using a rolling pin to transfer them from the work surface.

3. Divide the pizza sauce between the two pizza crusts, spreading almost to the edges. Top with the onion, pepperoni, mushrooms, and yellow bell pepper. Scatter over the cheese and season to taste with pepper.

4. Bake in the preheated oven for 10–12 minutes, or until the cheese is melting and golden and the crusts are crisp underneath. Serve immediately.

Makes 2 pizzas

1 quantity Basic Pizza Dough

1 tsp dried chile flakes

Topping

¾ cup prepared pizza sauce

1 red onion, finely sliced

7 oz/200 g hot pepperoni, thinly sliced

1½ cups thinly sliced button mushrooms

1 yellow pepper, seeded and thinly sliced

1¾ cups grated cheddar cheese or Monterey Jack cheese

pepper

77

Hamburger Pizza

1. Make the pizza dough as described on page 10. Punch down the dough by gently kneading for about a minute, then divide into two balls. Using a rolling pin, roll out each piece of dough to a 15 x 10½-inch/38 x 26-cm rectangle on a lightly floured work surface.

2. Preheat the broiler to high, place the hamburger patties on a broiler rack, and cook for 10–12 minutes, turning occasionally, until cooked through. Remove from the broiler and let cool slightly. Chop into bite-size chunks.

3. Preheat the oven to 425°F/220°C. Place each pizza crust on a 15 x 10½-inch/38 x 26-cm rectangular baking sheet, using a rolling pin to transfer them from the work surface.

4. Divide the pizza sauce between the two pizza crusts, spreading almost to the edges. Top with the hamburger chunks, onions, pickles, corn kernels, and cheese. Season to taste with salt and pepper.

5. Bake in the oven for 15–20 minutes, or until the cheese is melting and turning golden and the crusts are crisp underneath. Drizzle with the mustard and serve immediately.

Makes 2 large pizzas

✳ 2 quantities Basic Pizza Dough

Topping
4 large, lean hamburger patties
1½ cups prepared pizza sauce
2 red onions, finely sliced
1 cup roughly chopped pickles
½ cup drained canned corn kernels
7 oz/200 g cheese slices
salt and pepper
prepared mustard, to serve

Salmon & Sour Cream Pizza

1. Make the pizza dough as described on page 10. Punch down the dough by gently kneading for about a minute. Using a rolling pin, roll out the dough to a 15 x 10½-inch/38 x 26-cm rectangle on a lightly floured work surface.

2. Preheat the oven to 425°F/220°C. Place the pizza crust on a 15 x 10½-inch/38 x 26-cm rectangular baking sheet, using a rolling pin to transfer it from the work surface.

3. Brush the oil over the dough and season to taste with salt. Cover with a piece of parchment paper and a light baking sheet to prevent the dough from rising during cooking. Bake in the preheated oven for 8–10 minutes, then remove the paper and the sheet and cook for an additional 2–3 minutes, or until the dough is a light golden brown in color.

4. Remove from the oven and let cool for 5 minutes, then spread with the sour cream and scatter over the onion, chile, and salmon. Top with the tomatoes and dill and season to taste with pepper. Serve immediately with the lemon wedges for squeezing over.

Makes 1 large pizza

* 1 quantity Basic Pizza Dough

Topping
2 tbsp extra virgin olive oil

4 tbsp sour cream

1 red onion, finely chopped

1 red chile, seeded and finely chopped

7 oz/200 g smoked salmon, roughly sliced

2 tomatoes, finely sliced

1 tbsp finely chopped fresh dill

salt and pepper

lemon wedges, to serve

Asian Shrimp Pizza

1. Make the pizza dough as described on page 10. Punch down the dough by gently kneading for about a minute, then divide into two balls. To roll out the dough, flatten each ball, then, using a rolling pin, roll out on a lightly floured work surface, giving a quarter turn between each roll.

2. Preheat the oven to 425°F/220°C. Place the pizza crusts on two baking sheets, using a rolling pin to transfer them from the work surface.

3. Divide the salsa between the two pizza crusts, spreading almost to the edges. Scatter over the chiles, shrimp, lemongrass, scallions, and cheese. Season to taste with salt and pepper.

4. Bake in the preheated oven for 10–15 minutes, or until the cheese is melting and turning golden and the crusts are crisp underneath. Garnish with the fresh cilantro and serve immediately.

Makes 2 pizzas

* 1 quantity Basic Pizza Dough

Topping
¾ cup prepared tomato salsa
2 Thai chiles, seeded and finely chopped
5½ oz/150 g cooked jumbo shrimp, peeled
1 tsp finely chopped lemongrass
3 scallions, finely chopped
9 oz/250 g light mozzarella cheese, drained and roughly torn
salt and pepper
fresh cilantro, finely chopped, to garnish

80

Spicy Bean Feast Pizza

1. Make the pizza dough as described on page 10. Punch down the dough by gently kneading for about a minute, then divide into two balls. To roll out the dough, flatten each ball, then, using a rolling pin, roll out on a lightly floured work surface, giving a quarter turn between each roll.

2. Preheat the oven to 425°F/220°C. Place the pizza crusts on two baking sheets, using a rolling pin to transfer them from the work surface.

3. Heat the oil in a saucepan over medium heat. Add the onion and garlic and sauté for 4–5 minutes, until softened. Add the paprika and tomato paste and cook for 1–2 minutes, stirring continuously.

4. Add the chile flakes, beans, and pizza sauce and season to taste with salt and pepper. Bring to a fast simmer and cook, uncovered, for 10–15 minutes, until thickened and reduced.

5. Spread the bean mixture over the pizza crusts and top with the cheese.

6. Bake in the preheated oven for 10–15 minutes, or until the cheese is melting and turning golden and the crusts are crisp underneath. Garnish with the fresh parsley and serve immediately.

Makes 2 pizzas

* 1 quantity Basic Pizza Dough

Topping
1 tbsp olive oil
1 onion, finely chopped
2 garlic cloves, crushed
1 tsp smoked paprika
2 tbsp tomato paste
1 tsp dried chile flakes
1 cup drained and rinsed canned mixed beans
¾ cup prepared pizza sauce
2 cups grated low-fat cheddar cheese
salt and pepper
fresh flat-leaf parsley, roughly chopped, to garnish

Novelty

81

Three-Course Meal Pizza

1. Make the pizza dough as described on page 10. Punch down the dough by gently kneading for about a minute, then divide into two balls. To roll out the dough, flatten each ball, then, using a rolling pin, roll out on a lightly floured work surface, giving a quarter turn between each roll.

2. Preheat the oven to 425°F/220°C. Place the pizza crusts on two baking sheets, using a rolling pin to transfer them from the work surface.

3. Cover two-thirds of each crust with the pizza sauce, spreading almost to the edges, then spread the jelly on the remaining third.

4. Scatter the Parmesan cheese and olives over the first-third of each crust. Place the salami on the second-third of each crust, then top with the mozzarella cheese.

5. Spread mascarpone cheese over the jelly section of each crust, top with the peach slices, and sprinkle with the sugar.

6. Bake in the preheated oven for 10–12 minutes, or until the crusts are crisp underneath. Serve immediately.

Makes 2 pizzas

* 1 quantity Basic Pizza Dough

Topping
⅔ cup pizza sauce

4 tbsp raspberry jelly

¾ cup grated Parmesan cheese

4 black olives, pitted and halved

1 oz/30 g salami, chopped

1¾ oz/50 g mozzarella cheese, drained and coarsely torn

scant ½ cup mascarpone cheese

1 ripe peach, pitted and sliced into thin wedges

2 tbsp light brown sugar

82

Clock-Face Pizza

1. Make the pizza dough as described on page 10. Punch down the dough by gently kneading for about a minute, then divide into two balls. To roll out the dough, flatten each ball, then, using a rolling pin, roll out on a lightly floured work surface, giving a quarter turn between each roll.

2. Preheat the oven to 425°F/220°C. Place the pizza crusts on two baking sheets, using a rolling pin to transfer them from the work surface.

3. Divide the pizza sauce between the two pizza crusts, spreading almost to the edges. Scatter over the cheese.

4. To create the clock face on each crust, place a piece of ham at each numerical position of 12, 3, 6, and 9. Fill the spaces between each piece of ham with a green olive half.

5. For the clock hands, arrange the black olives in a line from the center of the pizza to the top edge, and in a second line from the center at a 90-degree angle from the first line.

6. Bake in the preheated oven for 10–12 minutes, or until the cheese is melting and turning golden and the crusts are crisp underneath. Serve immediately.

Makes 2 pizzas

1 quantity Basic Pizza Dough

Topping
¾ cup prepared pizza sauce

¾ cup grated cheddar cheese

1 slice cooked ham, cut into 1-inch/2.5-cm squares

4 green olives, pitted and halved

8 black olives, pitted and halved

Valentine Pizza

1. Make the pizza dough as described on page 10. Punch down the dough by gently kneading for about a minute, then divide into two balls. To roll out the dough, flatten each ball, then, using a rolling pin, roll out on a lightly floured work surface, giving a quarter turn between each roll. Using your hands, shape each piece of dough into a heart shape.

2. Preheat the oven to 400°F/200°C. Place the pizza crusts on two baking sheets, using a rolling pin to transfer them from the work surface.

3. Heat the vegetable oil in a skillet over medium–high heat. Add the scallops and bacon and sauté for 3–4 minutes. Remove from the skillet and drain on paper towels.

4. Divide the pizza sauce between the two crusts, spreading almost to the edges. Arrange the scallops and bacon evenly over the pizzas. Top with the cheese and season to taste with pepper.

5. Bake in the preheated oven for 10–15 minutes, or until the cheese is melting and turning golden and the crusts are crisp underneath. Pile the arugula onto the pizzas, add a drizzle of olive oil, and serve immediately.

Makes 2 pizzas

※ 1 quantity Basic Pizza Dough

Topping
1 tsp vegetable oil

3½ oz/100 g roeless scallops, halved horizontally

3½ oz/100 g Canadian bacon or smoked bacon, chopped

¾ cup prepared pizza sauce

7 oz/200 g Camembert cheese, sliced

pepper

fresh arugula leaves and extra virgin olive oil, to serve

Christmas Feast Pizza

1. Make the pizza dough as described on page 10. Punch down the dough by gently kneading for about a minute, then divide into two balls. To roll out the dough, flatten each ball, then, using a rolling pin, roll out on a lightly floured work surface, giving a quarter turn between each roll.

2. Preheat the oven to 425°F/220°C. Place the pizza crusts on two baking sheets, using a rolling pin to transfer them from the work surface.

3. Divide the cranberrry sauce between the two pizza crusts, spreading almost to the edges. Scatter over the turkey and top with all but 2 tablespoons of the cheese. Season to taste with pepper.

4. Bake in the preheated oven for 10–12 minutes, or until the cheese is melting and turning golden and the crusts are crisp underneath.

5. Let the pizzas cool slightly, then scatter with the reserved cheese. Serve immediately.

Makes 2 pizzas

* 1 quantity Basic Pizza Dough

Topping
scant 1 cup cranberry sauce
heaping 1 cup chopped,
   cooked turkey
¾ cup crumbled blue cheese
pepper

85

Mini Pizza Canapés

1. Make the pizza dough as described on page 10. Punch down the dough by gently kneading for about a minute. Divide the dough into 24 balls and, using a rolling pin, roll them into small, flat circles on a lightly floured work surface.

2. Preheat the oven to 375°F/190°C. Place the dough circles on several baking sheets. Lay a sheet of parchment paper over each sheet of pizza crusts and cover with a light baking sheet to prevent the dough from rising during cooking.

3. Bake in the preheated oven for 8–10 minutes, then remove the baking sheet and paper and return to the oven for an additional 5 minutes, or until they are light brown in color. Remove from the oven and let cool.

4. Spoon a little sour cream onto each pizza crust, then top with a piece of smoked salmon and season to taste with pepper. Garnish with the fresh chives and serve immediately.

Makes 24 mini pizzas

1 quantity Basic Pizza Dough

Topping
scant ½ cup sour cream
3½ oz/100 g smoked salmon pieces, rolled
pepper
finely snipped fresh chives, to garnish

Movie-Night-In Calzone

1. Make the pizza dough as described on page 10. Punch down the dough by gently kneading for about a minute, then divide into four balls. To roll out the dough, flatten each ball, then, using a rolling pin, roll out on a lightly floured work surface, giving a quarter turn between each roll. Roll each one to a circle with a diameter of about 7½ inches/19 cm.

2. Preheat the oven to 400°F/200°C. Place the pizza crusts on two baking sheets, using a rolling pin to transfer them from the work surface.

3. Heat the oil in a skillet over medium heat. Add the onion and sauté for 5–10 minutes, until golden and softened.

4. Divide the pizza sauce among the four pizza crusts, spreading almost to the edges then place equal amounts of frankfurter, onion, and cheese on half of each crust.

5. Brush the edges of the crusts with a little water, then fold them over the filling to make four half-moon-shape calzones. Seal the edges by folding a little of the dough over and pinching the edges together. Make small holes in the top of each calzone with the tip of a sharp knife.

6. Bake in the preheated oven for 10–15 minutes, or until the tops are golden and the crusts are crisp underneath. Serve immediately.

Makes 4 small calzones

1 quantity Basic Pizza Dough

Filling
1 tbsp vegetable oil
1 large red onion, finely sliced
¾ cup prepared pizza sauce
4 frankfurters, chopped
scant 1 cup grated smoked cheese

Children's Party Pizzas

1. Make the pizza dough as described on page 10. Punch down the dough by gently kneading for about a minute, then divide into four balls. To roll out the dough, flatten each ball, then, using a rolling pin, roll out on a lightly floured work surface, giving a quarter turn between each roll.

2. Preheat the oven to 425°F/220°C. Place the pizza crusts on two baking sheets, using a rolling pin to transfer them from the work surface. To shape the cat face, use your fingers to make two triangles in the top edge of each circle for ears.

3. Divide the pizza sauce among the four pizza crusts, spreading almost to the edges. Sprinkle over the cheese.

4. Use the olive halves to make the cats' eyes, rolled salami to make the whiskers, and some red bell pepper slices to make the mouth.

5. Bake in the preheated oven for 10–12 minutes, or until the cheese is melting and turning golden and the crusts are crisp underneath. Serve immediately.

Makes 4 small pizzas

1 quantity Basic Pizza Dough

Topping
¾ cup prepared pizza sauce

scant 1 cup grated mild cheddar cheese

4 black olives, pitted and halved

3 oz/85 g salami slices, rolled

1 red bell pepper, seeded and finely sliced

88

Mini Pinwheel Pizzas

1. Make the pizza dough as described on page 10. Punch down the dough by gently kneading for about a minute, then divide into two. Using a rolling pin, roll out each piece of dough on a lightly floured work surface to a 7 x 10-inch/ 18 x 25-cm rectangle.

2. Preheat the oven to 300°F/150°C. Place the pizza crusts on two 7 x 10-inch/18 x 25-cm rectangular baking sheets, using a rolling pin to transfer them from the work surface.

3. Divide the pizza sauce between the two pizza crusts, spreading to within 1¼ inches/3 cm at the top of the rectangle to let the topping move up slightly when you roll up the pizza from the opposite end.

4. Scatter the salami and cheese evenly over the crusts and season to taste with salt and pepper.

5. Make the pinwheel by tightly rolling the dough upward from the bottom toward the top end.

6. Using a pastry brush glaze the outside surface of the dough with the oil and cook in the preheated oven for 20–25 minutes, or until the dough is golden brown on top. Remove from the oven and cut each roll into eight slices, using a toothpick to secure each roll. Serve immediately.

Makes 2 pinwheel pizzas

✳ 1 quantity Basic Pizza Dough

Topping
¾ cup prepared pizza sauce
4 oz/115 g salami, chopped
5½ oz/150 g mozzarella cheese, drained and coarsely torn
salt and pepper
vegetable oil, to glaze

Shaped Pizzas

1. Make the pizza dough as described on page 10. Knock back the dough by gently kneading for about a minute, then divide into two balls. Using a rolling pin, roll out each ball on a lightly floured work surface. Form the dough into shapes of your choice, either by hand or with large, fun-shaped cookie cutters.

2. Preheat the oven to 425°F/220°C. Place the pizza crusts on two baking sheets, using a rolling pin to transfer them from the work surface.

3. Divide the barbecue sauce among the crusts, spreading almost to the edges. Scatter over the chicken and corn kernels and top with the cheese.

4. Place in the preheated oven for 10–12 minutes (slightly less for mini pizzas), or until the cheese is melting and turning golden and the crusts are crisp underneath. Serve immediately.

Makes 2 regular pizzas or several smaller pizzas

* 1 quantity Basic Pizza Dough

Topping
¾ cup prepared barbecue sauce

¾ cup sliced, cooked chicken

scant ½ cup drained canned corn kernels

¾ cup grated mild cheddar cheese

Brunch Special Calzone

1. Make the pizza dough as described on page 10. Punch down the dough by gently kneading for about a minute, then divide into two balls. To roll out the dough, flatten each ball, then, using a rolling pin, roll out on a lightly floured work surface, giving a quarter turn between each roll.

2. Preheat the oven to 400°F/200°C. Place the pizza crusts on two baking sheets, using a rolling pin to transfer them from the work surface.

3. Drain the baked beans through a strainer and put into a bowl, adding 2–3 tablespoons of the liquid. Add the bacon, mushrooms, and Worcestershire sauce and season to taste with salt and pepper.

4. Spread the mixture onto one-half of each of the crusts. Brush the edges of the crusts with a little water, then fold them over the filling to make two half-moon-shape calzones. Seal the edges by folding a little of the dough over and pinching the edges together. Make small holes in the top of each calzone with the tip of a sharp knife.

5. Bake in the preheated oven for 10–15 minutes, or until the tops are golden and the crusts are crisp underneath. Serve immediately.

Makes 2 calzones

✳ 1 quantity Basic Pizza Dough

Filling
scant 1 cup canned baked beans

3½ oz/100 g bacon slices, cooked and chopped

1½ cups thinly sliced mushrooms

dash Worcestershire sauce

salt and pepper

91

St. Patrick's Day Pizza

1. Make the pizza dough as described on page 10. Punch down the dough by gently kneading for about a minute, then divide into two balls. To roll out the dough, flatten each ball, then, using a rolling pin, roll out on a lightly floured work surface, giving a quarter turn between each roll.

2. Preheat the oven to 400°F/200°C. Place the pizza crusts on two baking sheets, using a rolling pin to transfer them from the work surface.

3. Divide the pizza sauce between the two pizza crusts, spreading almost to the edges. Scatter over the leek, corned beef, and corn kernels and top with the cheese. Season to taste with salt and pepper.

4. Bake in the preheated oven for 10–12 minutes, or until the cheese is melting and turning golden and the crusts are crisp underneath. Serve immediately.

Makes 2 pizzas

※ 1 quantity Basic Pizza Dough

Topping
¾ cup prepared pizza sauce

1 leek, finely chopped

5½ oz/150 g corned beef, chopped

⅔ cup drained canned corn kernels

1⅓ cups grated cheddar cheese

salt and pepper

Halloween Special Pizza

1. Make the pizza dough as described on page 10. Punch down the dough by gently kneading for about a minute, then divide into two balls. To roll out the dough, flatten each ball, then, using a rolling pin, roll out on a lightly floured work surface, giving a quarter turn between each roll.

2. Preheat the oven to 425°F/220°C. Place the pizza crusts on two baking sheets, using a rolling pin to transfer them from the work surface.

3. Place the pumpkin on a baking sheet, drizzle over the oil, and add the thyme. Season to taste with salt and pepper and toss well to coat. Place in the preheated oven and roast for 15 minutes, until softened and starting to char around the edges.

4. Divide the pizza sauce between the two pizza crusts, spreading almost to the edges. Scatter over the pumpkin and onion, then top with the cheese and season to taste with salt and pepper.

5. Return to the oven and bake for 10–12 minutes, or until the cheese is melting and turning golden and the crusts are crisp underneath. Serve immediately.

Makes 2 pizzas

✳ 1 quantity Basic Pizza Dough

Topping
3 cups diced pumpkin or butternut squash flesh
1 tbsp extra virgin olive oil
1 tsp dried thyme
¾ cup prepared pizza sauce
1 red onion, finely sliced
1 cup grated Gruyère cheese
salt and pepper

Apple Pie Pizza

1. Make the pizza dough as described on page 10, adding the cinnamon with the flour. Punch down the dough by gently kneading for about a minute, then divide into two balls. To roll out the dough, flatten each ball, then, using a rolling pin, roll out on a lightly floured work surface, giving a quarter turn between each roll.

2. Preheat the oven to 450°F/230°C. Place the pizza crusts on two baking sheets, using a rolling pin to transfer them from the work surface.

3. Melt the butter in a heavy-bottom nonstick skillet over medium heat. Add the sugar, stirring well to dissolve. Let bubble for 5–6 minutes, until dark and syrupy. Add the apples, raisins, and cloves and cook for an additional 4–5 minutes, until the apples are starting to soften but are not completely cooked.

4. Using a slotted spoon, divide the apple-and-raisin mixture between the two pizza crusts. Spoon over about half of the syrup, reserving the remainder.

5. Bake in the preheated oven for 8–10 minutes, or until the crusts are crisp underneath. Drizzle over the reserved syrup, dust with confectioners' sugar, and serve warm.

Makes 2 pizzas

✳ 1 quantity Basic Pizza Dough
1 tsp ground cinnamon

Topping
3 tbsp butter
½ cup light brown sugar
3 large apples, peeled, cored, and thickly sliced
⅓ cup raisins
pinch ground cloves
confectioners' sugar, for dusting

94

Chocolate, Banana & Berry Pizza

1. Make the pizza dough as described on page 10. Punch down the dough by gently kneading for about a minute, then divide into two balls. To roll out the dough, flatten each ball, then, using a rolling pin, roll out on a lightly floured work surface, giving a quarter turn between each roll.

2. Preheat the oven to 425°F/220°C. Place the pizza crusts on two baking sheets, using a rolling pin to transfer them from the work surface.

3. Divide the chocolate-and-hazelnut spread between the two pizza crusts, spreading almost to the edges. Top with the bananas and marshmallows.

4. Bake in the preheated oven for 8–10 minutes, or until the crusts are crisp underneath. Cover with foil for the last few minutes of cooking if the tops start to brown too much. Top with fresh berries and serve immediately.

Makes 2 pizzas

❋ 1 quantity Basic Pizza Dough

Topping
heaping ¾ cup chocolate-and-hazelnut spread
2 ripe bananas, peeled and thinly sliced
1 cup mini marshmallows
fresh berries, to serve

S'mores Special Pizza

① Make the pizza dough as described on page 10. Punch down the dough by gently kneading for about a minute, then divide into two balls. To roll out the dough, flatten each ball, then, using a rolling pin, roll out on a lightly floured work surface, giving a quarter turn between each roll.

② Preheat the oven to 425°F/220°C. Place the pizza crusts on two baking sheets, using a rolling pin to transfer them from the work surface.

③ Divide the chocolate spread between the two pizza crusts, spreading almost to the edges. Top with the cookies, marshmallows, and chocolate chunks.

④ Bake in the preheated oven for 8–10 minutes, or until the crusts are crisp underneath. Cover with foil for the last few minutes of cooking if the tops start to brown too much. Dust with confectioners' sugar and serve warm with the mascarpone cheese, if using.

Makes 2 pizzas

✳ 1 quantity Basic Pizza Dough

Topping
6 tbsp chocolate spread

3½ oz/100 g chocolate chip cookies, coarsely chopped

1 cup mini marshmallows

3 oz/85 g milk chocolate, broken into chunks

confectioners' sugar, for dusting

¾ cup mascarpone cheese, to serve (optional)

96

Caramelized Plum Pizza

1. Make the pizza dough as described on page 10. Punch down the dough by gently kneading for about a minute, then divide into two balls. To roll out the dough, flatten each ball, then, using a rolling pin, roll out on a lightly floured work surface, giving a quarter turn between each roll.

2. Preheat the oven to 425°F/220°C. Place the pizza crusts on two baking sheets, using a rolling pin to transfer them from the work surface.

3. Melt the butter in a heavy-bottom nonstick skillet over medium heat. Add the sugar, stirring well to dissolve. Let bubble for 5–6 minutes, until dark and syrupy. Add the sliced plums and cook for an additional 3–4 minutes, until they are starting to soften but are not completely cooked.

4. Using a slotted spoon, divide the plums evenly over the pizza crusts. Drizzle over half of the syrup.

5. Bake in the preheated oven for 8–10 minutes, or until the crusts are crisp underneath. Drizzle over the reserved syrup, dust with confectioners' sugar, and serve warm with the mascarpone cheese.

Makes 2 pizzas

1 quantity Basic Pizza Dough

Topping
4 tbsp butter

¾ cup light brown sugar

8 ripe purple plums, halved, pitted, and sliced

confectioners' sugar, for dusting

¾ cup mascarpone cheese, to serve

97

Thanksgiving Pizza

1. Make the pizza dough as described on page 10. Punch down the dough by gently kneading for about a minute, then divide into two balls. To roll out the dough, flatten each ball, then, using a rolling pin, roll out on a lightly floured work surface, giving a quarter turn between each roll.

2. Preheat the oven to 425°F/220°C. Place the pizza crusts on two baking sheets, using a rolling pin to transfer them from the work surface.

3. Divide the pizza sauce between the two pizza crusts, spreading almost to the edges. Mix the stuffing with the red currant sauce and crumble over the pizza crusts. Top with the turkey and cheese and season to taste with salt and pepper.

4. Bake in the preheated oven for 10–12 minutes, or until the cheese is melting and turning golden and the crusts are crisp underneath. Garnish with the chopped parsley and serve immediately.

Makes 2 pizzas

* 1 quantity Basic Pizza Dough

Topping
¾ cup prepared pizza sauce
1 cup prepared stuffing
4 tbsp red currant sauce
1 cup shredded, cooked turkey
1¾ cups grated Gruyère cheese
salt and pepper
chopped fresh flat-leaf parsley, to garnish

98

Cherry Pie &
Mascarpone Pizza

1. Make the pizza dough as described on page 10. Punch down the dough by gently kneading for about a minute, then divide into two balls. To roll out the dough, flatten each ball, then, using a rolling pin, roll out on a lightly floured work surface, giving a quarter turn between each roll.

2. Preheat the oven to 425°F/220°C. Place the pizza crusts on two baking sheets, using a rolling pin to transfer them from the work surface.

3. Cover each crust with a piece of parchment paper and a light baking sheet to prevent the dough from rising during cooking. Bake in the preheated oven for 8–10 minutes, then remove the baking sheet and paper and return to the oven for an additional 3–5 minutes, or until lightly browned.

4. Spread the mascarpone cheese evenly over the pizza crusts and spoon over the cherry pie filling. Dust generously with confectioners' sugar and serve immediately.

Makes 2 pizzas

* 1 quantity Basic Pizza Dough

Topping
¾ cup mascarpone cheese
¾ cup canned cherry pie filling, warmed
confectioners' sugar, for dusting

Strawberry & Ricotta Cheese Pizza

1. Make the pizza dough as described on page 10. Punch down the dough by gently kneading for about a minute, then divide into two balls. To roll out the dough, flatten each ball, then, using a rolling pin, roll out on a lightly floured work surface, giving a quarter turn between each roll.

2. Preheat the oven to 425°F/220°C. Place the pizza crusts on two baking sheets, using a rolling pin to transfer them from the work surface.

3. Brush the crusts evenly with the honey. Using a fork, pierce the dough in several places to prevent it from rising during cooking. Bake in the preheated oven for 10–12 minutes, until golden brown and bubbling.

4. Scatter over the strawberries and spoon over the ricotta cheese. Dust generously with confectioners' sugar and serve immediately.

Makes 2 pizzas

* 1 quantity Basic Pizza Dough

Topping
6 tbsp honey

2½ cups hulled and quartered strawberries

6 tbsp ricotta cheese

confectioners' sugar, for dusting

Greek Salad Pizza

1. Make the pizza dough as described on page 10. Punch down the dough by gently kneading for about a minute, then divide into two balls. To roll out the dough, flatten each ball, then, using a rolling pin, roll out on a lightly floured work surface, giving a quarter turn between each roll.

2. Preheat the oven to 425°F/220°C. Place the pizza crusts on two baking sheets, using a rolling pin to transfer them from the work surface.

3. Spray the top of the crusts with the oil spray, scatter over 2 teaspoons of the oregano, and season to taste with salt and pepper. Cover each crust with a piece of parchment paper and a light baking sheet to prevent the dough from rising during cooking.

4. Bake in the preheated oven for 8–10 minutes, or until lightly browned, then remove the baking sheets and paper and return to the oven for an additional 3–5 minutes.

5. Mix the remaining ingredients for the salad topping in a bowl and season to taste with salt and pepper. Spoon over the warm pizza crusts and serve immediately.

Makes 2 pizzas

* 1 quantity Basic Pizza Dough

Topping
extra virgin olive oil spray
3 tsp finely chopped fresh oregano
6 cherry tomatoes, halved
½ cucumber, peeled, seeded, and thinly sliced
¼ cup halved, pitted black olives
⅔ cup drained and crumbled feta cheese
1 small red onion, finely sliced
1 tbsp extra virgin olive oil
squeeze of fresh lemon juice
salt and pepper

Apple Pie Pizza 206
artichoke hearts
    Artichoke & Brie Pizza 25
    Artichoke Pizza 88
    Chorizo, Artichoke & Olive Pizza 158
    Salami & Artichoke Pizza 76
    Sicilian Pizza 22
    Vegetable Lovers Pizza 37
arugula
    Grilled Sirloin & Blue Cheese Pizza 86
    Melted Brie & Bacon Pizza 68
    Prosciutto & Arugula Pizza 64
    Smoked Salmon & Dill Pizza 98
    Valentine Pizza 187
Asian Shrimp Pizza 176
asparagus
    Crab, Asparagus & Ricotta Cheese Pizza 115
    Roasted Red Pepper & Asparagus Pizza 40
    Vegetable Lovers Pizza 37

bacon
    Brunch Special Calzone 200
    Canadian Bacon, Baked Egg & Mozzarella Pizza 62
    Melted Brie & Bacon Pizza 68
    Monkfish & Bacon Pizza 116
    Valentine Pizza 187
baked beans: Brunch Special Calzone 200
bananas: Chocolate, Banana & Berry Pizza 208
barbecue sauce
    Barbecued Chicken Pizza 67
    Shaped Pizzas 199
Barbecued Chicken Pizza 67
basil
    Marinara Calzone 122
    Mozzarella & Basil Pizza 50
    Pesto & Ricotta Cheese Pizza 49
    Pizza Margherita 14
    Pizza Neapolitan 44
    Tuna, Olive & Ricotta Cheese Pizza 109
beans
    Brunch Special Calzone 200
    Chili con Carne Calzone 152
    Pizza Mexicana 157
    Spicy Bean Feast Pizza 178
beef
    Chili con Carne Calzone 152
    Grilled Sirloin & Blue Cheese Pizza 86
    Hamburger Pizza 172
    Peppered Steak Pizza 169
    Piccante Pizza 61
    Pizza Mexicana 157
    St Patrick's Day Pizza 202
    Triple Chile Pizza 140
bell peppers
    Barbecued Chicken Pizza 67
    Cajun-Spiced Chicken Pizza 154
    Chicken & Salsa Pizza 79
    Chicken & Spinach Pizza 92
    Children's Party Pizzas 194
    Chile-Crusted Pepperoni Pizza 170
    Chorizo & Manchego Pizza 73
    Clam & Green Pepper Pizza 133
    Crab, Gruyère Cheese & Spinach Pizza 112
    Fajita-Style Chicken Pizza 166
    Hawaiian Shrimp Pizza 128
    Meat Feast Pizza 56
    Monkfish & Bacon Pizza 116
    Pepperoni & Jalapeño Pizza 74
    Piccante Pizza 61
    Pizza Mexicana 157
    Pork Meatball Pizza 160
    Roasted Red Pepper & Asparagus Pizza 40
    Salami & Artichoke Pizza 76

Sicilian Pizza 22
    Smoked Ham, Mushroom & Ricotta Cheese Pizza 94
    Spicy Bell Peppers & Goat Cheese Pizza 142
    Spicy Chicken Pizza 151
    Spicy Shrimp Salsa Pizza 104
    Triple Chile Pizza 140
    see also chiles; jalapeño peppers
berries
    Chocolate, Banana & Berry Pizza 208
    Strawberry & Ricotta Cheese Pizza 218
Blue Cheese & Pear Pizza 43
Brie
    Artichoke & Brie Pizza 25
    Four Cheese Pizza 28
    Melted Brie & Bacon Pizza 68
Brunch Special Calzone 200
butternut squash: Halloween Special Pizza 205

Cajun-Spiced Chicken Pizza 154
calzone
    Brunch Special Calzone 200
    Chili con Carne Calzone 152
    Garlic, Shrimp & Mushroom Calzone 130
    Marinara Calzone 122
    Movie-Night-In Calzone 193
    Sun-Dried Tomato & Ricotta Cheese Calzone 32
    Tuna, Fennel & Red Onion Calzone 106
Canadian Bacon, Baked Egg & Mozzarella Pizza 62
capers
    Pine Nut & Raisin Pizza 31
    Sicilian Pizza 22
    Smoked Salmon with Spinach & Capers Pizza 100
Caramelized Plum Pizza 212
Caramelized Red Onion & Fennel Pizza 38
cheese
    Barbecued Chicken Pizza 67
    Blue Cheese & Pear Pizza 43
    Caramelized Red Onion & Fennel Pizza 38
    Children's Party Pizzas 194
    Chile-Crusted Pepperoni Pizza 170
    Chili Crab with Mussels Pizza 118
    Chorizo & Manchego Pizza 73
    Chorizo, Artichoke & Olive Pizza 158
    Christmas Feast Pizza 188
    Clock-Face Pizza 184
    Fajita-Style Chicken Pizza 166
    Four Cheese Pizza 28
    Grilled Sirloin & Blue Cheese Pizza 86
    Hamburger Pizza 172
    Hawaiian Pizza 58
    Hot Dog & Mustard Pizza 164
    Indian-Style Pizza 146
    Meat Feast Pizza 56
    Monkfish & Bacon Pizza 116
    Movie-Night-In Calzone 193
    Peppered Steak Pizza 169
    Pepperoni & Jalapeño Pizza 74
    Piccante Pizza 61
    Pizza Mexicana 157
    Pork Meatball Pizza 160
    St Patrick's Day Pizza 202
    Shaped Pizzas 199
    Spicy Bean Feast Pizza 178
    Tilapia with Sharp Cheddar & Red Onion Pizza 124
    Triple Chile Pizza 140
    Tuna, Fennel & Red Onion Calzone 106
    Valentine Pizza 187
    see also Brie; feta cheese; goat cheese; Gruyère cheese;
        mascarpone cheese; mozzarella cheese; Parmesan cheese;
        ricotta cheese
Cherry Pie & Mascarpone Pizza 217
chicken
    Barbecued Chicken Pizza 67
    Cajun-Spiced Chicken Pizza 154

Chicken & Salsa Pizza 79
    Chicken & Spinach Pizza 92
    Fajita-Style Chicken Pizza 166
    Indian-Style Pizza 146
    Pesto Chicken Pizza 82
    Shaped Pizzas 199
    Spicy Chicken Pizza 151
Children's Party Pizzas 194
chiles
    Asian Shrimp Pizza 176
    Chile Tuna Pizza 110
    Chile-Crusted Pepperoni Pizza 170
    Chili con Carne Calzone 152
    Chili Crab with Mussels Pizza 118
    Indian-Style Pizza 146
    Mussel & Caramelized Fennel Pizza 127
    Piccante Pizza 61
    Pizza Mexicana 157
    Pork Meatball Pizza 160
    Salmon & Sour Cream Pizza 175
    Spicy Bean Feast Pizza 178
    Spicy Bell Peppers & Goat Cheese Pizza 142
    Spicy Mozzarella Pizza 34
    Spicy Shrimp Salsa Pizza 104
    Tapenade & Mozzarella Pizza 145
    Thai Chile Shrimp Pizza 163
    Triple Chile Pizza 140
    see also jalapeño peppers
chocolate
    Chocolate, Banana & Berry Pizza 208
    S'mores Special Pizza 211
chorizo
    Chorizo & Manchego Pizza 73
    Chorizo, Artichoke & Olive Pizza 158
    Spanish Spicy Pizza 148
Christmas Feast Pizza 188
cilantro
    Asian Shrimp Pizza 176
    Hawaiian Shrimp Pizza 128
    Indian-Style Pizza 146
    Jumbo Shrimp & Cilantro Pesto Pizza 134
    Pizza Mexicana 157
    Clam & Green Pepper Pizza 133
    Clock-Face Pizza 184
corn
    Chile Tuna Pizza 110
    Garlic, Shrimp & Mushroom Calzone 130
    Hamburger Pizza 172
    Pesto Chicken Pizza 82
    St Patrick's Day Pizza 202
    Shaped Pizzas 199
corned beef: St Patrick's Day Pizza 202
crabmeat
    Chili Crab with Mussels Pizza 118
    Crab, Asparagus & Ricotta Cheese Pizza 115
    Crab, Gruyère Cheese & Spinach Pizza 112
cranberry sauce: Christmas Feast Pizza 188
cucumber
    Duck & Plum Sauce Pizza 85
    Greek Salad Pizza 220

dill
    Salmon & Sour Cream Pizza 175
    Smoked Salmon & Dill Pizza 98
dough 7–8
    Basic Pizza Dough 10
    kneading 7–8
    rolling out 8
dried fruit
    Apple Pie Pizza 206
    Pine Nut & Raisin Pizza 31
Duck & Plum Sauce Pizza 85

eggplants
    The Greek Pizza 91
    Vegetable & Goat Cheese Pizza 16
eggs
    Canadian Bacon, Baked Egg & Mozzarella Pizza 62
    Spinach, Egg & Olive Pizza 20

Fajita-Style Chicken Pizza 166
fennel
    Caramelized Red Onion & Fennel Pizza 38
    Mussel & Caramelized Fennel Pizza 127
    Tuna, Fennel & Red Onion Calzone 106
feta cheese
    The Greek Pizza 91
    Greek Salad Pizza 220
    Grilled Zucchini & Feta Pizza 46
fish & seafood
    Asian Shrimp Pizza 176
    Chile Tuna Pizza 110
    Chili Crab with Mussels Pizza 118
    Clam & Green Pepper Pizza 133
    Crab, Asparagus & Ricotta Cheese Pizza 115
    Crab, Gruyère Cheese & Spinach Pizza 112
    Garlic, Shrimp & Mushroom Calzone 130
    Hawaiian Shrimp Pizza 128
    Jumbo Shrimp & Cilantro Pesto Pizza 134
    Marinara Calzone 122
    Mini Pizza Canapés 190
    Monkfish & Bacon Pizza 116
    Mussel & Caramelized Fennel Pizza 127
    Salmon & Sour Cream Pizza 175
    Scallop, Pea, Leek & Lemon Pizza 136
    Seafood Pizza 121
    Smoked Salmon & Dill Pizza 98
    Smoked Salmon with Spinach & Capers Pizza 100
    Spicy Shrimp Salsa Pizza 104
    Sushi-Style Smoked Salmon with Wasabi Pizza 103
    Thai Chile Shrimp Pizza 163
    Tilapia with Sharp Cheddar & Red Onion Pizza 124
    Tuna, Fennel & Red Onion Calzone 106
    Tuna, Olive & Ricotta Cheese Pizza 109
    Valentine Pizza 187
Four Cheese Pizza 28
frankfurters
    Hot Dog & Mustard Pizza 164
    Movie-Night-In Calzone 193

garlic
    Artichoke Pizza 88
    Cajun-Spiced Chicken Pizza 154
    Garlic Bread 8
    Garlic, Mushroom & Gruyère Pizza 26
    Garlic, Shrimp & Mushroom Calzone 130
    The Greek Pizza 91
    Grilled Zucchini & Feta Pizza 46
    Mussel & Caramelized Fennel Pizza 127
    Piccante Pizza 61
    Pizza Margherita 14
    Pizza Mexicana 157
    Pizza Neapolitan 44
    Pork Meatball Pizza 160
    Potato & Rosemary Pizza 52
    Spicy Bean Feast Pizza 178
    Spicy Bell Peppers & Goat Cheese Pizza 142
    Spinach, Egg & Olive Pizza 20
    Vegetable & Goat Cheese Pizza 16
ginger
    Spicy Chicken Pizza 151
    Sushi-Style Smoked Salmon with Wasabi Pizza 103
goat cheese
    Goat Cheese & Olive Pizza 19
    Potato & Rosemary Pizza 52
    Salami & Artichoke Pizza 76

    Spicy Bell Peppers & Goat Cheese Pizza 142
    Vegetable & Goat Cheese Pizza 16
The Greek Pizza 91
Greek Salad Pizza 220
Grilled Sirloin & Blue Cheese Pizza 86
Grilled Zucchini & Feta Pizza 46
Gruyère cheese
    Crab, Gruyère Cheese & Spinach Pizza 112
    Garlic, Mushroom & Gruyère Pizza 26
    Halloween Special Pizza 205
    Thanksgiving Pizza 214

Halloween Special Pizza 205
ham
    Artichoke Pizza 88
    Clock-Face Pizza 184
    Ham, Mushroom & Olive Pizza 80
    Hawaiian Pizza 58
    Meat Feast Pizza 56
    Smoked Ham, Mushroom & Ricotta Cheese Pizza 94
    see also prosciutto
Hamburger Pizza 172
harissa paste: Thai Chile Shrimp Pizza 163
Hawaiian Pizza 58
Hawaiian Shrimp Pizza 128
helpful hints 8
honey
    Spicy Chicken Pizza 151
    Strawberry & Ricotta Cheese Pizza 218

Indian-Style Pizza 146
Italian Meat Special Pizza 70

jalapeño peppers
    Chicken & Salsa Pizza 79
    Pepperoni & Jalapeño Pizza 74
    Pizza Mexicana 157
    Triple Chile Pizza 140
jelly: Three-Course Meal Pizza 182
Jumbo Shrimp & Cilantro Pesto Pizza 134

kidney beans: Chili con Carne Calzone 152
kneading dough 7-8

lamb: The Greek Pizza 91
leeks
    St Patrick's Day Pizza 202
    Scallop, Pea, Leek & Lemon Pizza 136
lemons: Scallop, Pea, Leek & Lemon Pizza 136

Marinara Calzone 122
marshmallows
    Chocolate, Banana & Berry Pizza 208
    S'mores Special Pizza 211
mascarpone cheese
    Caramelized Plum Pizza 212
    Cherry Pie & Mascarpone Pizza 217
    S'mores Special Pizza 211
    Three-Course Meal Pizza 182
Meat Feast Pizza 56
Melted Brie & Bacon Pizza 68
Mini Pinwheel Pizzas 196
Mini Pizza Canapés 190
Monkfish & Bacon Pizza 116
Movie-Night-In Calzone 193
mozzarella cheese
    Artichoke Pizza 88
    Asian Shrimp Pizza 176
    Barbecued Chicken Pizza 67
    Cajun-Spiced Chicken Pizza 154
    Canadian Bacon, Baked Egg & Mozzarella Pizza 62
    Chicken & Salsa Pizza 79
    Chicken & Spinach Pizza 92

    Chile Tuna Pizza 110
    Chorizo, Artichoke & Olive Pizza 158
    Clam & Green Pepper Pizza 133
    Four Cheese Pizza 28
    Garlic, Shrimp & Mushroom Calzone 130
    Ham, Mushroom & Olive Pizza 80
    Hawaiian Pizza 58
    Hawaiian Shrimp Pizza 128
    Italian Meat Special Pizza 70
    Marinara Calzone 122
    Mini Pinwheel Pizzas 196
    Mozzarella & Basil Pizza 50
    Mussel & Caramelized Fennel Pizza 127
    Pesto Chicken Pizza 82
    Piccante Pizza 61
    Pine Nut & Raisin Pizza 31
    Pizza Margherita 14
    Prosciutto & Arugula Pizza 64
    Roasted Red Pepper & Asparagus Pizza 40
    Scallop, Pea, Leek & Lemon Pizza 136
    Seafood Pizza 121
    Sicilian Pizza 22
    Smoked Salmon with Spinach & Capers Pizza 100
    Spanish Spicy Pizza 148
    Spicy Chicken Pizza 151
    Spicy Mozzarella Pizza 34
    Tapenade & Mozzarella Pizza 145
    Thai Chile Shrimp Pizza 163
    Three-Course Meal Pizza 182
    Vegetable Lovers Pizza 37
mushrooms
    Brunch Special Calzone 200
    Chile Tuna Pizza 110
    Chile-Crusted Pepperoni Pizza 170
    Garlic, Mushroom & Gruyère Pizza 26
    Garlic, Shrimp & Mushroom Calzone 130
    Ham, Mushroom & Olive Pizza 80
    Meat Feast Pizza 56
    Sicilian Pizza 22
    Smoked Ham, Mushroom & Ricotta Cheese Pizza 94
    Vegetable Lovers Pizza 37
mussels
    Chili Crab with Mussels Pizza 118
    Marinara Calzone 122
    Mussel & Caramelized Fennel Pizza 127
    Seafood Pizza 121

olives
    Artichoke Pizza 88
    Children's Party Pizzas 194
    Chorizo & Manchego Pizza 73
    Chorizo, Artichoke & Olive Pizza 158
    Clock-Face Pizza 184
    Goat Cheese & Olive Pizza 19
    Greek Salad Pizza 220
    Ham, Mushroom & Olive Pizza 80
    Italian Meat Special Pizza 70
    Prosciutto & Arugula Pizza 64
    Sicilian Pizza 22
    Spanish Spicy Pizza 148
    Spicy Mozzarella Pizza 34
    Spinach, Egg & Olive Pizza 20
    Three-Course Meal Pizza 182
    Tuna, Olive & Ricotta Cheese Pizza 109
    Vegetable Lovers Pizza 37
onions
    Chili con Carne Calzone 152
    The Greek Pizza 91
    Hot Dog & Mustard Pizza 164
    Piccante Pizza 61
    Pizza Mexicana 157
    Pork Meatball Pizza 160
    Spicy Bean Feast Pizza 178

Spicy Bell Peppers & Goat Cheese Pizza 142
see also red onions; spring onions
oregano
Cajun-Spiced Chicken Pizza 154
Clam & Green Pepper Pizza 133
The Greek Pizza 91
Greek Salad Pizza 220
Italian Meat Special Pizza 70
Salami & Artichoke Pizza 76
Spicy Chicken Pizza 151
Tapenade & Mozzarella Pizza 145

Parmesan cheese
Artichoke Pizza 88
Clam & Green Pepper Pizza 133
Jumbo Shrimp & Cilantro Pesto Pizza 134
Mussel & Caramelized Fennel Pizza 127
Pesto & Ricotta Cheese Pizza 49
Pizza Margherita 14
Seafood Pizza 121
Spicy Shrimp Salsa Pizza 104
Spinach, Egg & Olive Pizza 20
Three-Course Meal Pizza 182
pastrami: Meat Feast Pizza 56
peaches: Three-Course Meal Pizza 182
pears: Blue Cheese & Pear Pizza 43
peas: Scallop, Pea, Leek & Lemon Pizza 136
Peppered Steak Pizza 169
pepperoni
Chile-Crusted Pepperoni Pizza 170
Meat Feast Pizza 56
Pepperoni & Jalapeño Pizza 74
pesto
Indian-Style Pizza 146
Jumbo Shrimp & Cilantro Pesto Pizza 134
Pesto & Ricotta Cheese Pizza 49
Pesto Chicken Pizza 82
Smoked Ham, Mushroom & Ricotta Cheese Pizza 94
Piccante Pizza 61
pickles: Hamburger Pizza 172
pine nuts
The Greek Pizza 91
Pine Nut & Raisin Pizza 31
pineapple
Hawaiian Pizza 58
Hawaiian Shrimp Pizza 128
pizza peel 8
Pizza Sauce Recipe 9
pizza stone 8
plums
Caramelized Plum Pizza 212
Duck & Plum Sauce Pizza 85
Pork Meatball Pizza 160
Potato & Rosemary Pizza 52
prosciutto
Italian Meat Special Pizza 70
Prosciutto & Arugula Pizza 64
Spanish Spicy Pizza 148
pumpkin: Halloween Special Pizza 205

red currant sauce: Thanksgiving Pizza 214
red onions
Artichoke & Brie Pizza 25
Cajun-Spiced Chicken Pizza 154
Caramelized Red Onion & Fennel Pizza 38
Chile-Crusted Pepperoni Pizza 170
Clam & Green Pepper Pizza 133
Crab, Asparagus & Ricotta Cheese Pizza 115
Fajita-Style Chicken Pizza 166
Greek Salad Pizza 220
Halloween Special Pizza 205
Hamburger Pizza 172
Movie-Night-In Calzone 193
Mussel & Caramelized Fennel Pizza 127
Peppered Steak Pizza 169

Pepperoni & Jalapeño Pizza 74
Pine Nut & Raisin Pizza 31
Potato & Rosemary Pizza 52
Salmon & Sour Cream Pizza 175
Seafood Pizza 121
Sicilian Pizza 22
Smoked Ham, Mushroom & Ricotta Cheese Pizza 94
Spicy Chicken Pizza 151
Spicy Mozzarella Pizza 34
Tapenade & Mozzarella Pizza 145
Tilapia with Sharp Cheddar & Red Onion Pizza 124
Tuna, Fennel & Red Onion Calzone 106
ricotta cheese
Crab, Asparagus & Ricotta Cheese Pizza 115
Pesto & Ricotta Cheese Pizza 49
Smoked Ham, Mushroom & Ricotta Cheese Pizza 94
Smoked Salmon & Dill Pizza 98
Strawberry & Ricotta Cheese Pizza 218
Sun-Dried Tomato & Ricotta Cheese Calzone 32
Sushi-Style Smoked Salmon with Wasabi Pizza 103
Tuna, Olive & Ricotta Cheese Pizza 109
Roasted Red Pepper & Asparagus Pizza 40
rosemary
Potato & Rosemary Pizza 52
Seafood Pizza 121

St Patrick's Day Pizza 202
salami
Children's Party Pizzas 194
Italian Meat Special Pizza 70
Mini Pinwheel Pizzas 196
Salami & Artichoke Pizza 76
Three-Course Meal Pizza 182
see also pepperoni
Salmon & Sour Cream Pizza 175
scallions
Asian Shrimp Pizza 176
Barbecued Chicken Pizza 67
Chili Crab with Mussels Pizza 118
Duck & Plum Sauce Pizza 85
Indian-Style Pizza 146
Jumbo Shrimp & Cilantro Pesto Pizza 134
Spicy Shrimp Salsa Pizza 104
Sushi-Style Smoked Salmon with Wasabi Pizza 103
Thai Chile Shrimp Pizza 163
scallops
Scallop, Pea, Leek & Lemon Pizza 136
Valentine Pizza 187
Seafood Pizza 121
Shaped Pizzas 199
shrimp
Asian Shrimp Pizza 176
Garlic, Shrimp & Mushroom Calzone 130
Hawaiian Shrimp Pizza 128
Jumbo Shrimp & Cilantro Pesto Pizza 134
Marinara Calzone 122
Seafood Pizza 121
Spicy Shrimp Salsa Pizza 104
Thai Chile Shrimp Pizza 163
Sicilian Pizza 22
Smoked Ham, Mushroom & Ricotta Cheese Pizza 94
smoked paprika
Fajita-Style Chicken Pizza 166
Spanish Spicy Pizza 148
Spicy Bean Feast Pizza 178
smoked salmon
Mini Pizza Canapés 190
Salmon & Sour Cream Pizza 175
Smoked Salmon & Dill Pizza 98
Smoked Salmon with Spinach & Capers Pizza 100
Sushi-Style Smoked Salmon with Wasabi Pizza 103
S'mores Special Pizza 211
sour cream
Fajita-Style Chicken Pizza 166
Mini Pizza Canapés 190

Peppered Steak Pizza 169
Salmon & Sour Cream Pizza 175
Spicy Chicken Pizza 151
Spanish Spicy Pizza 148
Spicy Bean Feast Pizza 178
Spicy Bell Peppers & Goat Cheese Pizza 142
Spicy Chicken Pizza 151
Spicy Mozzarella Pizza 34
Spicy Shrimp Salsa Pizza 104
spinach
Chicken & Spinach Pizza 92
Crab, Gruyère Cheese & Spinach Pizza 112
Smoked Salmon with Spinach & Capers Pizza 100
Spinach, Egg & Olive Pizza 20
squid
Marinara Calzone 122
Seafood Pizza 121
strawberries: Strawberry & Ricotta Cheese Pizza 218
Sun-Dried Tomato & Ricotta Cheese Calzone 32
Sushi-Style Smoked Salmon with Wasabi Pizza 103

Tapenade & Mozzarella Pizza 145
Thai Chile Shrimp Pizza 163
Thanksgiving Pizza 214
Three-Course Meal Pizza 182
thyme
Artichoke & Brie Pizza 25
Halloween Special Pizza 205
Tilapia with Sharp Cheddar & Red Onion Pizza 124
tomatoes
Artichoke Pizza 88
Asian Shrimp Pizza 176
Chile Tuna Pizza 110
Chili con Carne Calzone 152
Chili Crab with Mussels Pizza 118
Goat Cheese & Olive Pizza 19
Greek Salad Pizza 220
Grilled Sirloin & Blue Cheese Pizza 86
Hawaiian Shrimp Pizza 128
Mozzarella & Basil Pizza 50
Pesto & Ricotta Cheese Pizza 49
Pesto Chicken Pizza 82
Pizza Neapolitan 44
Pizza Sauce Recipe 9
Salmon & Sour Cream Pizza 175
Spicy Shrimp Salsa Pizza 104
Sun-Dried Tomato & Ricotta Cheese Calzone 32
Tapenade & Mozzarella Pizza 145
Triple Chile Pizza 140
Tuna, Olive & Ricotta Cheese Pizza 109
Vegetable Lovers Pizza 37
Triple Chile Pizza 140
tuna
Chile Tuna Pizza 110
Tuna, Fennel & Red Onion Calzone 106
Tuna, Olive & Ricotta Cheese Pizza 109
turkey
Christmas Feast Pizza 188
Smoked Ham, Mushroom & Ricotta Cheese Pizza 94
Thanksgiving Pizza 214
tzatziki: The Greek Pizza 91

Valentine Pizza 187
Vegetable & Goat Cheese Pizza 16
Vegetable Lovers Pizza 37

wasabi sauce: Sushi-Style Smoked Salmon with Wasabi Pizza 103

yeast 7

zucchini
Grilled Zucchini & Feta Pizza 46
Vegetable & Goat Cheese Pizza 16